CW00954195

Homemade Healthy Dog Food Cookbook

An Easy-to-Follow Guide and Collection of the Best Recipes to Make Your Dog Happy and Healthy

Table of Contents

Introduction

If you are reading this book, it's because you are thinking seriously about your dog's health and want to find a better, healthier way to feed him. Or you may have already made the decision to feed your dog homemade food but don't know where to start.

Millions of people worldwide are busy right now creating tasty meals for their best pal, all in the comfort of their own kitchen. It's not difficult – apart from raw food, anything you cook for your dog is perfectly safe for human consumption, making it healthier than anything you can buy in a pet or grocery store.

This is the only book you will ever need to get your dog on the right track to a healthy, long, and happy life. The healthier and happier your dog is, the longer you get to spend time with your best friend, and the more adventures and fun you can have.

This is an easy-to-read book packed with useful information that tells you exactly why you should be making your dog's food. It walks you through the nutritional value of homemade food, what you should and shouldn't feed your dog, and provides you with plenty of easy-to-make recipes that will delight your dog and won't take you long to make.

It is the ideal book for beginners, as it explains things in simple language with plenty of step-by-step instructions and pictures to help you along the way.

This is one of the most exciting journeys you will ever take and the difference you will see in your dog will make it all worthwhile. So let's not waste any more time. Turn the pages and learn why homemade food for dogs is the only way to go.

Chapter 1: Making Homemade Food for Your Dog

More and more people are turning their backs on packaged, pre-made dog food in favor of homemade, but why? It's well known that many of the major dog food brands have been recalled at one time or another, but are they really that unhealthy? The answer to that question is no. They are not. Provided your dog is fed a balanced diet, it doesn't matter what you feed it. However, homemade food offers benefits that far surpass the convenience of commercial foods.

1.   *More dog owners are turning their backs on premade food. Source: https://www.pexels.com/photo/dog-food-in-a-stainless-steel-bowl-8434641/*

Why Make Your Own Dog Food?

Without a doubt, you have been shocked by the price rises in commercial dog food recently, and you're not alone in thinking it must be cheaper to make your own food at home. You're absolutely right, but there is more to it. By making your own dog food, you know exactly what your dog is eating, and that's something you can't know when you feed them a commercial diet. Dry kibble and tinned dog meats may contain real meat, but not much of it, and they are also jam-packed with preservatives, coloring, flavoring, and even unhealthy fillers. You don't get any of that with homemade food.

The most difficult part about making your own dog food is taking that first step. Once you make the decision to do it, it only gets easier. And the biggest reward is in knowing that you are changing your dog's life for the better.

Think about the benefits from your dog's point of view:

- The food is tastier and even fussy, picky eaters will love what you put in front of them.

- You control the ingredients, so they get to enjoy a wide range of meats, grains, fruits, veggies, and more, all safe for them to eat.

- They don't get food packed with artificial ingredients.

Here are three of the best reasons to make your own food:

1. **The tools available make it dead simple:** So many kitchen tools are available now that making dog food at home is dead simple. Slow cookers, electric pressure cookers, food processors, and more have all

made life so much easier and more precise than ever before in prepping dog food.

2. **It can be cheaper:** Obviously, if you are feeding your dog the cheapest kibble, homemade food won't be any cheaper. But if you are feeding your best friend on one of the premium foods, you know that they don't come cheap. You may even have tried home-delivered fresh foods, which aren't cheap, either. If you love looking for bargains in the grocery stores and you grow your own fruit and veg, there are plenty of savings to be made.

3. **It's healthier and better for your dog:** Much of today's commercial food is of somewhat questionable quality, and that's because it has to be mass-produced while still meeting safety requirements. The ingredients are cooked at incredibly high temperatures to kill off bacteria, but this also kills off the natural goodness in them, like the minerals and vitamins your dog needs. Thos have been replaced with artificial supplements, which don't always offer what they should. Making your own dog food ensures you use the highest quality ingredients and provide a perfect, nutritionally balanced meal for your dog to enjoy.

The Caveats

Before deciding whether making your own dog food is better, you need to understand some of the misconceptions surrounding it.

Some people will tell you there's no way you can provide the balanced nutrition that commercial food does, but you absolutely can. All dogs need a balance of carbs, protein, fat, minerals, and vitamins, and that's easy to provide in a freshly made meal.

Others will tell you that you shouldn't change your dog's diet because it can be dangerous. While you certainly should make a sudden and complete change all at once, it is easy enough to transition your dog onto a homemade diet, and doing it right is not dangerous. In fact, your dog will love you for it, as it benefits them in so many ways.

That said, there are caveats to this, as with everything.

In the same way that humans may be sensitive or allergic to certain ingredients, dogs can, too. The usual culprits are protein, wheat, and eggs, so always begin with a short but basic list of ingredients. Try things slowly and monitor your dog. If they get diarrhea, start scratching themselves constantly, or suffer itchy ears, you'll be able to find what caused it easier than if you use an ingredient list longer than a best-selling novel. Also, if your dog has an existing medical condition that needs a special diet, i.e., kidney disease, or is a puppy or senior, you should consult your veterinarian to ensure you make the right food.

Aside from those, you'll find cooking your dog's meals is incredibly meaningful and you know that you are doing the best for your pet's health. Your dog will welcome the fresh ingredients and appreciate every mouthful of his delicious food.

Equipment

2.   The first step towards committing to homemade dogfood is getting the right equipment. Source: https://www.pexels.com/photo/a-woman-putting-the-green-leaves-and-strawberries-in-the-blender-8845657/

One of the best things you can do is have a plan, which means having the right ingredients and tools to make whatever you want. You will need certain kitchen appliances, such as:

Prep:

- Accurate kitchen scales
- Food blender
- Food processor
- Food-safe tubs
- Grinder – for bones and meat
- Kitchen scissors
- Mixing bowls (stainless steel is best)
- Sharp knives

- Wood chopping boards

Storage:

- Food-safe plastic containers (freezer-safe)
- Freezer
- Glass containers
- Ice cube trays
- Parchment paper
- Silicon molds
- Silicon storage bags

Cleaning:

- Cleaning wipes
- Disinfectant
- Natural disinfectant and cleaning sprays

Have a separate space set up in your kitchen, and ensure that you don't mix up your utensils and equipment with those you use for dog food. Yes, this does mean having a specific blender, food processor, etc., just for dog food, but it's worth it. Also, ensure you disinfect everything before and after – including work surfaces.

The Health Benefits of Homemade Dog Food

When you look at commercial dog food packaging, do you look for labeling that tells you it is wholesome, healthy, nutritious food? Sure you do, we all do. But just because the packaging tells you something, doesn't mean it is true. More often than not, labeling is misleading, and it doesn't mean one food is any better than another.

You've heard people tell you that you are what you eat, and the same applies to dogs. You need to consider a bag of commercial dog food akin to a box of fast food, perhaps fries and a burger. If a human eats fast food every day, they'll certainly not be healthy, but if they eat a wholesome diet packed with protein, veggies, fruits, and grains, they'll feel better and look better. The same happens with dogs fed on a commercial diet, but the difference is noticeable when switching them to a homemade, fresh food diet.

Here are ten reasons fresh, homemade food can improve your best pal's health and well-being:

1. It Reduces the Risks of Common Medical Conditions

Homemade dog food high in good quality proteins and antioxidants keeps several conditions away. As with humans, good nutrition is key to reversing some symptoms or even preventing diseases from appearing in the first place. A study published in the JAVMA (Journal of American Veterinary Medical Association) found that when Scottish terriers ate a diet containing orange-yellow, leafy, and green veggies three times weekly, they had a much lower risk of bladder carcinoma than those who didn't.

Most commercial foods are full of poor-quality ingredients that aren't fit for human consumption. Why are these ingredients rejected for human consumption? Mostly because animals are disabled or already dying by the time they reach the slaughterhouse, or the grains were filthy from being in the dirt on the floor and therefore not fit for humans. But these reasons apparently make it okay for animals to eat. And that's not the worst of it. Those ingredients are then combined with fake vitamins, unhealthy fillers, dyes, preservatives, and more. This kind of food is bad for your dog, hard to digest, and causes all sorts of gastrointestinal and other problems.

2. It Helps Your Dog Stay at a Healthy Weight

It is down to you to ensure your dog's weight is healthy and it is nearly always in your control. According to a survey of vets, only around 3% of canine obesity cases were due to factors such as illness or genetic abnormalities. The rest were down to a lack of exercise and a poor diet.

3. A good diet means a healthy dog. Source:
https://www.pexels.com/photo/dog-with-ball-in-mouth-jumping-over-a-fallen-tree-trunk-3013467/

Commercial dog foods are the main culprit, packed as they are with starches – ingredients used to keep costs down. Most dog food contains poor-quality fillers, such as potato, rice, and wheat, and while these can be a great addition to your dog's diet, they should be used properly and in accordance with a completely homemade diet. You know it yourself – if you eat a starchy, high-carb diet, the weight piles on, and it's not easy to shift it.

Freshly prepped dog food is balanced – a combination of nutrient-dense, lightly cooked ingredients – that prevents your dog from gaining weight while keeping them healthy inside and out.

3. It Can Help Your Dog Live Longer

One study found that dogs consuming a fresh, homemade diet lived longer than those fed on a commercial diet, by as much as three to four years, proving that homemade diets are generally healthier.

The synthetic ingredients in commercial food all take their toll on your dog, reducing their lifespan and making them generally unwell. You could easily live on nothing more than junk food, but you wouldn't live long, and your risks for disease and early death would be much higher. The same applies to your dog. Feed them a commercial diet for too long and it will affect them in more ways than one.

4. It's Better for Their Digestive Health

Your dog's gut needs the right balance of nutrients to stay healthy and work as it should. That should be a balance of meat and vegetables, a diet that has endured for ventures. Wild dogs would kill and eat small prey, but they wouldn't just eat the meat and bones; they also consumed the stomach contents, which normally consisted of grass and vegetation. This meant the dog would get a good amount of veggies rich in fiber and nutrients, keeping their digestion in good working order. You can feed your dog the same kind of diet and improve their digestive health.

5. It Gives Them Healthy Poop

If you feed your dog a commercial diet, you've probably noticed that they poop a lot, and it smells! You will notice a huge difference when you switch to a fresh, homemade diet.

Their bowel movements will be smaller, more consistent, and less smelly. That's because homemade foods are packed with healthy fiber, something every person and every animal needs to keep their digestive system moving.

6. It Helps Them Sleep Better

When your dog has a healthy digestive system, they will sleep better. Dogs who constantly pace, sigh or keep changing position usually have an upset digestive system, so feeding them a homemade diet fixes that, making them feel better overall and leading to better, less disturbed sleep.

7. It Helps Their Cognitive Functioning and Learning

A healthy diet and brain health have long been linked in humans, and the same applies to dogs. A study was done on senior dogs with poor cognitive functioning. They were given a det rich in antioxidants and showed significant improvements in brain-derived neurotrophic factors. Their levels were much higher, thus slowing down the rate of cognitive decline. But it's not just senior dogs who should be fed this kind of diet. Feeding younger dogs on an antioxidant-rich diet can help improve their alertness and learning functions.

8. It Improves The Condition of Their Coat

Itchy, dry skin, scabs, and rashes are common in dogs these days, and most of the time, they are given steroids and cortisone shots to treat those problems. Those medications all come with their own potentially dangerous side effects, thus making things worse. Vets will tell owners that their dog has an allergy of some kind but, more often than not, it is down to a dietary deficiency. Commercial foods are full of unhealthy fillers and other poor ingredients that don't give your dog the nutrition they need. Dried food is cooked at high temperatures, killing all the nutrients and goodness and doesn't contain the oils and healthy fats needed for healthy skin and a moisturized coat.

4.   It gives them a healthier coat. Source: https://www.pexels.com/photo/a-woman-sitting-on-a-couch-playing-with-her-dog-4680240/

Switch your dog to a fresh, homemade diet, and within a matter of days, you will see a significant improvement in their skin and coat. If this doesn't happen, it may be that they do have an allergy, one of the most common of which is chicken. The easiest way to find out if your dog has an allergy is to switch to another protein source. It is rare for dogs to be allergic to all proteins, so you will find one that works for you and your dog.

9. It Gives Them Energy and Helps in Recovery After Exercise

All dogs need regular exercise, be it a walk in the woods or something more taxing, like agility. That means they require the right fuel to help them exercise, and that comes from a healthy, balanced, nutritious diet. High-quality protein gives your dog the energy they need, keeping them happy and strong during their exercise. Fresh protein also helps your dog's muscles recover quicker after exercise, meaning they are more than ready for their next walk.

10.   It Can Help Picky Eaters

Some dogs are fussy about what they eat, and who can blame them – commercial food doesn't always smell that great to humans, and dogs have more sensitive noses, so they can smell more. A fresh homemade diet smells better and is more enticing to a younger, picky dog, while older dogs will find it easier to eat – softer foods don't need so much chewing. Fresh food also has a higher water content, so your dog will stay hydrated longer.

Charts and Conversions

When making your own dog food, you will need to know how to convert measurements, especially if you need to make more or less than the recipe. The following charts will help you do this easily:

Liquid Conversions

1 fluid ounce	2 tablespoons
1 cup	8 fluid ounces
1 pint	16 fluid ounces OR 2 cups
1 quart	2 fluid ounces OR 2 pints
1 gallon	128 fluid ounces OR 4 quarts

Dry Conversions

1 tablespoon	3 teaspoons
¼ cup	4 tablespoons
1/3 cup	5 tablespoons + 1 teaspoon
½ cup	8 tablespoons
1 cup	16 tablespoons

Measuring Cups and Spoons

Most of the time, you can buy measuring cups and spoons in complete sets, but knowing the order by size is still helpful.

Cups:

- 1/8 cup
- ¼ cup
- 1/3 cup
- ½ cup
- 1 cup

Spoons:

- ¼ tsp
- ½ tsp
- 1 tsp
- ½ tbsp
- 1 tbsp

Metric to Imperial

Sometimes, a recipe will not be in measurements you use, i.e., if you are used to using imperial measurements but the recipe is in metric. The following charts can help you make the right conversion:

Oven Temperatures:

Celsius – Electric	Celsius – Fan	Fahrenheit	Gas
120°	100°	250°	1
150°	130°	300°	2
160°	140°	325°	3
180°	160°	350°	4
190°	170°	375°	5
200°	180°	400°	6
230°	210°	450°	7
250°	230°	500°	9

Fan ovens tend to cook quicker, so adjust your cooking time accordingly.

Cups and Spoons

Imperial	Metric
¼ cup	60 ml

1/3 cup	80 ml
½ cup	125 ml
1 cup	250 ml
¼ teaspoon	1.25 ml
½ teaspoon	2.5 ml
1 teaspoon	5 ml
2 teaspoons	10 ml
1 tablespoon (4 teaspoons)	20 ml

Liquid Conversions

Metric	Cups	Imperial
30 ml		1 fluid ounce
60 ml	¼ cup	2 fluid ounces
80 ml	1/3 cup	2 ¾ fluid ounces
100 ml		3 ½ fluid ounces
125 ml	½ cup	4 fluid ounces
150 ml		5 fluid ounces
180 ml	¾ cup	6 fluid ounces
200 ml		7 fluid ounces

250 ml	1 cup	8 ¾ fluid ounces
310 ml	1 ¼ cups	10 ½ fluid ounces
375 ml	1 ½ cups	13 fluid ounces
430 ml	1 ¾ cups	15 fluid ounces
475 ml		16 fluid ounces
500 ml	2 cups	17 fluid ounces
625 ml	2 ½ cups	21 ½ fluid ounces
750 ml	3 cups	26 fluid ounces
1 liter	4 cups	35 fluid ounces
1 ¼ liters	5 cups	44 fluid ounces
1 ½ liters	6 cups	52 fluid ounces
2 liters	8 cups	70 fluid ounces
2 ½ liters	10 cups	88 fluid ounces

Weight (Mass)

Grams	Ounces/Pounds
10 grams	¼ ounce
15 grams	½ ounce
30 grams	1 ounce

60 grams	2 ounces
90 grams	3 ounces
125 grams	4 ounces OR ¼ lb.
155 grams	5 ounces
185 grams	6 ounces
220 grams	7 ounces
250 grams	8 ounces OR ½ lb.
280 grams	9 ounces
315 grams	10 ounces
345 grams	11 ounces
375 grams	12 ounces OR ¾ lb.
410 grams	13 ounces
440 grams	14 ounces
470 grams	15 ounces
500 grams OR ½ kilogram	16 ounces OR 1 lb.
750 grams	24 ounces OR 1 ½ lb.
1000 grams OR 1 kilogram	32 ounces OR 2 lb.

1500 grams OR 1 ½ kilograms	48 ounces OR 3 lb.
2000 grams OR 2 kilograms	64 ounces OR 4 lb.

Dog-Safe Foods and What to Avoid

5. You need to know what food, fruits and vegetables are safe for your dog to eat. Source: https://www.pexels.com/photo/black-berries-with-sliced-fruits-on-white-plate-87583/

You've taken the hardest step – deciding to switch your dog to a fresh, homemade diet. Now comes the next hardest part – making sure you feed them on safe foods. Dogs need a balanced diet but also variety, so they don't get bored and to give them the widest range of nutrients possible. The following is a list of the best dog-safe foods to feed your best friend:

- **Apples:** Full of fiber and crunch, apples help keep your dog's teeth clean and are full of vitamins A and C, which help their immune system and bones. However, you always core apples to remove the seeds, as these may be poisonous to dogs.

- **Blueberries:** These may be small, but they are one of the most powerful antioxidants you can feed your dog, and they are full of fiber. They are good for helping prevent disease and keep cells healthy.

- **Butternut Squash:** Packed with potassium, fiber, vitamin A, and vitamin C, butternut squash is great for digestive health and boosting the immune system.

- **Cooked Vegetables:** Veggies are packed with fiber and are a godsend to your dog's digestive health. They are also full of vitamins and minerals but use a variety to ensure your dog gets a good range and cook them without adding seasoning or salt.

- **Eggs:** Packed with protein, eggs are great for helping your dog's tissues repair and feed their muscles. It doesn't matter how you cook them – poached, scrambled, boiled, etc., so long as you don't cook them with butter.

- **Fish:** Preferably oily fish like tuna, salmon, and sardines, as these offer high levels of omega-3s that improve skin and coat health. They also help brain health, which makes fish a great choice for any dog, no matter their age,

- **Ground Eggshells:** This can give a much-needed calcium boost to dogs that need it. Ground eggshells can help strengthen teeth and bones, but you should use organic eggs where you can. Store-bought eggs are sometimes cleaned using a bleach solution, which can harm your dog's health.

- **Lettuce:** Low in calories, lettuce is perfect for training and as a low-calorie snack for obese dogs.

- **Meat:** Including chicken, beef, lamb, and turkey, meat provides the amino acids and proteins dogs need for energy and good, strong muscles. They should be well cooked without bones – never feed your dog cooked bones, as they can splinter and cause serious damage.

- **Oatmeal:** This is good for senior dogs and those who suffer irregular bowel movements. It also provides energy but should be cooked plain, with no added extras.

- **Peanut Butter:** An excellent source of healthy fat and protein, but make sure you use a xylitol-free variety, as xylitol is poisonous to dogs.

- **Plain Yogurt:** A lovely treat, yogurt is full of probiotics to help your dog's digestive functioning. It must be plain and must not contain added extras like sweeteners.

- **Pumpkin and Sweet Potatoes:** Orange foods are excellent for the digestive system and offer your dog many different vitamins and nutrients.

- **Raw Broccoli:** This is full of fiber and vitamins but be careful how much you use. Too much raw broccoli can cause digestive upset, negating the health benefits of feeding a homemade diet and causing your dog unnecessary pain.

- **Zucchini:** Packed with nutrients, zucchini offers minerals and vitamins, boosts the immune system, and helps improve skin and coat health.

Every dog has different nutritional needs, so make sure you introduce new foods gradually and keep an eye on your dog to see what, if any, changes occur. You should also ensure that you feed your dog a balance of these foods, as each one on its own is not a replacement for a meal. Provided you feed your dog a healthy, nutritious balance of foods, your dog will have a healthy, long, and happy life.

Food to Avoid

While there are many human foods your dog can safely enjoy, there are also plenty that can do them harm. Understanding which foods to avoid feeding your dog is paramount to their health, well-being, and your own well-being and pocket!

Dogs do not metabolize their food the same way humans do. What might seem like a tasty treat to you can cause problems for your dog, from a mildly upset stomach to more series issues, including death. Dogs don't always care what they eat, and some will eat anything they can get their teeth into. That means it is your responsibility to keep unsafe foods out of their reach.

6.   Chocolate can be extremely harmful to a dog's digestive system.
Source: https://unsplash.com/photos/brown-chocolate-bar-on-
black-table-uNi4M3sHqOo

These are the worst foods you can feed your dog:

- **Raisins and Grapes:** These are well known to have an adverse effect on kidney health and can cause kidney failure. Signs to look out for are lack of energy and vomiting.

- **Chocolate:** Human chocolate is full of caffeine and theobromine, which can cause all sorts of issues in dogs, including mild vomiting, seizures, and, in severe cases, death.

- **Alliums:** This includes chives, leeks, onions, and garlic. These are an irritant and can cause problems in the gut, and they can destroy red blood cells, causing anemia.

- **Xylitol:** This is often a major ingredient in sugar-free foods and is dangerous to dogs. It can cause spikes in insulin, leading to liver failure, and can cause their blood sugar to drop suddenly.

- **Alcohol:** Even the smallest quantity of alcohol can be toxic to dogs and can lead to coma and death.

- **Caffeine:** Never give your dog caffeinated coffee, tea, or any other drink with caffeine in it, as it can be fatal. It can make them restless, speed up their breathing, and cause tremors in their muscles.

- **Cooked Bones:** Cooked bones are harder than raw and can splinter, causing choking and internal damage.

- **Avocado:** The pit and skin are full of persin, which can cause diarrhea and vomiting. However, you can feed your dog very small amounts of the flesh, as it doesn't contain enough persin to worry.

- **Macadamia Nuts:** These can lead to fever, vomiting, and weakness.

- **Yeast Dough:** This can expand in the stomach very quickly, leading to bloating, and it can cause twisting in the stomach, which is potentially lethal.

- **Salty Food:** Too much salt can cause seizures and vomiting and affect your dog's health in many other ways.

- **Milk:** It's surprising how many dogs are lactose intolerant and cannot digest milk or milk products as it causes too much trouble with the digestive system. However, other dairy products, like plain yogurt, are much easier to digest and easier for the dog to handle.

- **Corn on the Cob:** while this is not in any way toxic, it can lead to blockages in the intestine.

Some dogs may not have any serious issues resulting from eating any of these foods, but others will. It's best to avoid them altogether to mitigate the risks.

A Guide to Buying the Right Ingredients

When you shop for your dogs, keep two things in mind: purity and freshness. Each ingredient is key to creating a nutritional powerhouse to keep your dog healthy.

Protein is one of the main ingredients, and the right variety is important. Ground meats and chicken breast are staple ingredients, but you should also include organ meats, like hearts, gizzards, and livers, as they are nutritious. You may not find these freely in your local store, but you can get them easily.

Find your local ethnic stores for the experience and the wide range of foods you can find in them. Or head to a farmer's market. While you may not see displays of organ meats, you could make an arrangement with one of the farmers or butchers for those they have too much of.

You could also join a raw food cooperative and join other like-minded people in purchasing bulk supplies, thus saving everyone money. However, do make sure you have freezer space first.

Fresh fruits and veggies are usually seasonal, but you can use frozen varieties. These are picked immediately when they are at their freshest and frozen, locking in the nutrition. Use fresh, in-season ingredients where you can and frozen varieties the rest of the time. Alternatively, you could grow your own. Things like spinach are easy to grow, and you don't need a vast amount of space. If you use frozen, read the labels to ensure they don't contain added seasonings and sugar.

Where some items are truly seasonal and you can't buy them any other time of the year, stock up when they are abundant in the shops and freeze them immediately. That way, you have access to what you want all the year.

The Right Meat

The primary ingredient in homemade dog food is cooked or raw meat, as dogs need a good protein source and are classed as obligate carnivores – this means they need meat for their nutrients as they can't get everything from plant foods.

7. *Always buy fresh meat that you would use for yourself. Source: https://unsplash.com/photos/sliced-meat-on-brown-wooden-chopping-board-yizdlpAds9c*

Always use fresh meat that is fit for humans, with a fat content of roughly 8 to 15%. Here are the best mats:

- **Beef:** Use ground, lean stewing meat, boneless roast joints, boneless steak, and hearts.

- **Lamb:** Use boneless, ground stewing meat, butt, leg, and shank.

- **Poultry:** Use skinless, boneless breasts and thighs. You can also use lean ground poultry meat, so long as it has no bone.

- **Venison:** Use ground boneless stewing meat, shoulder, shank, and necks.

You should also consider using rabbit, elk, caribou, moose, buffalo, duck, or small amounts of pork.

Raw fish can lead to a deficiency in thiamine, so keep it to a minimum and stick to oily sources, such as wild-caught, salmon, sardines, and tuna.

Vegetables

Dogs can eat most vegetables, and these should make up roughly one-quarter of each meal. They are packed with fiber, minerals, and vitamins, but for your dog to get the most benefit, they should be chopped, lightly steamed, or pureed, never cooked at high temperatures for long periods, as this destroys the nutrients.

That was quite a packed chapter, but you now have a great starting point. You know why you should be feeding your dog homemade fresh food, and you know what to feed them, so let's move on to structuring their meals.

Chapter 2: Easy Recipes for Protein-Packed Main Meals

Like humans, dogs have certain nutritional needs, but these needs are rarely met with commercially prepared foods. Nutrition is key to health, and feeding your pooch the right food ensures they stay healthy and live a longer, happier life. The key to this is feeding them a healthy, nutritionally balanced diet.

8. *It's easy to design fun and healthy meals with the right ingredients.*
    Source: https://unsplash.com/photos/white-and-brown-english-
    bulldog-on-brown-wooden-table-RCDcigzmtII

Designing Balanced Meals

The important ingredients for your dog are as follows:

Protein:

Proteins provide the dog with the amino acids his body cannot produce, which is critical for creating glucose for energy. Sources include boneless, skinless poultry, with all visible fat removed, beef, lamb, fish, and small amounts of pork.

Fats/Fatty Acids:

Plant seed oils and animal fats provide the best concentrated fat sources your dog needs, and a decent diet provides the fatty acids not produced in his body. Fatty acids keep the cells healthy and structurally sound, keep the coat and skin healthy, and make food taste better. The best sources are plant-based oils and fish oils.

Carbs:

Some carbs are required for energy, and the best sources are quinoa, pasta, rice, and oatmeal.

Fiber:

This is needed to keep the digestive system running smoothly and help them maintain a healthy weight. The best sources are pumpkins, apples, brown rice, dark leafy greens, carrots, and flaxseed.

Vitamins:

Dogs need vitamins for growth and body maintenance, and deficiencies can lead to many different health issues. That said, too many can also be dangerous. The best sources for the vitamins dogs require are:

- **Vitamin A:** Pumpkin and carrots
- **B Vitamins:** Green veggies, liver, and whole grains
- **Vitamin C:** Veggies, fruits, organ meats
- **Vitamin D:** Beef, fish, and liver
- **Vitamin E:** Liver, plant-based oils, leafy green veggies, and bran
- **Vitamin K:** Fish and leafy green veggies
- **Choline:** Egg yolks, meat, fish, and liver

Minerals:

Dogs also require 12 minerals for good health:

- **Calcium:** Cauliflower, broccoli, green beans, and tofu – strong teeth and bones
- **Phosphorus:** Eggs and meat – strong teeth and bones
- **Magnesium, Sodium, Potassium, and Chloride:** Whole grains, veggies, and fruit – transmission of nerve impulses, cell signaling, and muscle contraction
- **Sulfur:** Molasses, meat, and fish – for healthy nails, coat, and skin
- **Iron:** Poultry and red meat – boosts the immune system and supports red blood cells
- **Iodine:** Seafood, kelp, and dairy – healthy thyroid
- **Zinc:** Lamb, eggs, brewer's yeast, and liver – boosts the immune system and keeps the coat and skin healthy
- **Selenium:** Brown rice, seafood, veggies and meat – for the immune system

- **Copper:** Seeds, whole grains, and seafood

Water:

One thing that often gets overlooked, but water is a vital component in your dog's diet. While a fresh, homemade diet has more water than a commercial dry food, you should always ensure your dog has a plentiful supply of fresh drinking water at all times.

9. Water is a crucial part of any dog's diet. Source: https://www.flickr.com/photos/133374862@N02/20503577545

How to Structure Your Dog's Meals

Knowing what to include in your dog's diet is one thing. Knowing the ratios of proteins, fats, carbs, and fiber is another thing entirely. Let's look at the best ratios:

- **Muscle Meat:** 40 to 60% of their diet, providing proteins and fats. Try chicken, lamb, beef, and turkey to give your dog variety.

- **Fish:** 10% of their diet – not for every meal. Fish is packed with omega- and fatty acids for healthy skin and coat, and for good joints and healthy cognitive functioning.

- **Organ Meat:** 10 to 20% of their diet, providing minerals and vitamins, Green tripe, liver, and heart are the best sources.

- **Carbs:** 10 to 20% of their diet and should be healthy sources, like butternut squash and sweet potato. Dogs cannot digest carbs like humans and don't need so much.

- **Raw Meaty Bones:** 10% of their diet, or you can use ground eggshells as an alternative. These are packed with calcium and help keep their teeth clean.

- **Veggies and fruits:** 10 to 20% of their diet, providing minerals, vitamins, and fiber to keep your dog healthy inside out.

- **Seeds and Oils:** 1 to 2% of their diet, only a small part but critical as they add micronutrients and fatty acids. The best sources are fish, krill, and plant-based oils like olive, coconut, safflower, hempseed, and sesame. You can also add ground seeds, including chia, hemp, pumpkin, and flax.

- **Supplements:** 1% of their diet, ensuring complete nutrition.

Structuring your dog's meals in this way ensures they are getting the best nutrition every time. Don't forget that while carbs can be included, it shouldn't be to the extent that they overshadow the proteins, which are the more important part of the food.

Common Feeding Mistakes to Avoid

Feeding your dog correctly is the only way to give them the nutrients they need. However, it is a learning curve and there are some mistakes commonly made by beginners. Before learning those mistakes, you must understand that every dog is different, and every meal must be tailored to your dog's needs. This is especially important if you have more than one dog, as you may need to prepare completely different meals for each one, especially if one or more already has a medical complaint. Let's look at those common mistakes:

1. Feeding Too Much

This is by far the most common error and the biggest cause of obesity in dogs, which, as we all know, can lead to other health conditions. Most dogs will not stop eating when they have had enough – they will continue until the bowl is empty. Don't forget that their wild ancestors would do this because they didn't know where their next meal was coming from, but that isn't true of your dog. It's down to you to make sure your dog is only fed as much as they need, no more.

2. Not Including Treats in the Daily Meal Plan

Treats are fine in moderation, but not when you don't consider them in the overall food supply for the day. When you give your dog a treat, deduct it from the daily food quantity, ensuring your dog doesn't overeat. If you don't and continue feeding your dog full meals, you'll soon notice the weight is piling on, especially if they don't exercise enough.

3. Not Feeding Enough

Overfeeding your dog is bad, but so is underfeeding them. If you don't provide enough food, your dog's energy levels will drop, they will lose weight and can become listless. It also means they are not getting the nutrients they need, which comes with its own set of problems.

4. Using Grease and Oil to Supplement the Food

Many people are under the common misconception that they should add copious amounts of oil to their dog's food, mostly because they think it will do them good. The consequences are not nice – diarrhea and far more bowel movements than normal. That extra oil is unnecessary if you feed your dog a nutritionally complete meal. If you need to supplement with oil, make sure you only use a little of it and only use high-quality fish or plant oils.

5. Not Supplying the Right Amounts of Minerals

Another common error is not feeding your dog the right levels of minerals. These are just as important as protein, carbs, and fats, especially selenium, phosphorus, and calcium, the latter of which is important for bone and teeth health. However, so is phosphorus, and getting the balance right between the two is not always easy, but it is critical. Selenium supports the immune system, along with the metabolism of carbs and thyroid health. Over or under-supplying these minerals can cause health issues for your dog, sometimes serious, so getting the dosage right is critical.

6. Feeding Harmful Food

Most dogs are more than just a furry pet. They are a member of your family and your best friend and deserve the best care possible. However, that doesn't mean you should spoil them, especially when it involves giving them harmful food. You might think that a grape or a square of chocolate can do no harm, but you would be wrong. If you want to reward your dog, use healthy snacks that are counted as part of their daily meal plan.

7. Feeding Spoiled Food

When you make dog food in bulk, it can easily spoil if it isn't stored properly, like a sack of dog biscuits can spoil if left open and unused for long periods. Some foods are also contaminated with bacteria, including bull pizzle and pig ears, both touted as healthy treats. Spoiled food can upset the digestive system in a dog, the same as it does with humans, and in your dog's case, it can also lead to serious illness. Make sure you only feed high-quality, fresh food, and if you make it in bulk, ensure it is stored properly to keep it safe.

8. Feeding Too Many Supplements

Many dog owners think that if they feed their dogs a ton of supplements, they are only doing them good. This is not the case. Your dog shouldn't need supplements if fed a nutritionally balanced meal. However, some can be helpful for certain health complaints – turmeric is good for joint pain and arthritis. You must also be aware of compatibility issues between certain supplements, as incompatibility will negate all your good efforts. As a rule, you should only use supplements when there is a real need for them, and make sure they are given in the correct dosage.

Making these mistakes can be serious in terms of your dog's health, especially when you continuously make the same ones. Only feeding the right amount of quality food can ensure your dog remains healthy and happy.

Adjusting Meals for Different Dog Breeds and Sizes

10. Dogs come in different breeds and sizes, and each have different diet requirements. Source: https://unsplash.com/photos/a-couple-of-dogs-that-are-on-a-leash-xu2C-Ev7iRA

How much you feed your dog depends on several things:

- **Breed:** Smaller breeds don't eat as much as larger breeds. For example, you wouldn't feed an adult Chihuahua the same amount as an adult German Shepherd.

- **Age:** Puppies and younger dogs need the calories to help them grow and are usually fed more food and more frequently than adults, while senior dogs don't eat so much.

- **Activity:** Working or active dogs need to eat more to fulfill their energy needs. If your dog has a lot of exercise or does agility training, feed them more.

- **Health:** Some diseases can affect appetite and metabolism, including hypothyroidism. You should get assistance from your vet to see if anything is wrong before you change your dog's diet.

How Often Should Dogs Eat?

One of the essential things is to get your dog into a feeding routine. This ensures their health, but it does depend on the breed:

- **Small Breeds:** Such as Chihuahuas, Pomeranians, etc. The best feeding routine is two or three smaller meals daily, and that's because smaller dogs have smaller stomachs and a high metabolism, which means they need food more often. Feeding them two or three smaller meals keeps their blood sugar stable and provides the energy they need.

- **Medium Breeds:** Such as Bulldogs, Beagles, etc. These should normally be fed twice daily, so work out their daily allowance and divide it into two. Depending on their activity, feed them one portion in the morning and the other in the evening.

- **Large Breeds:** Such as German Shepherds, Retrievers, Labradors, etc. Their metabolism is slower, so two meals a day is sufficient, and they should be equally spaced to ensure the dog can digest their food properly and use the energy well.

- **Giant Breeds:** Such as Sant Bernards, Great Danes, etc. Because of their huge size, giant breeds have special nutritional requirements and may need to be fed up to four times a day. However, as they get older, that can be reduced.

Some people prefer only to feed their dogs once a day, but this won't always provide everything your dog needs. It can result in behavioral problems and upset stomachs, so try to feed your dog to a routine, and don't underfeed them.

In setting a routine, try to stick to the same times every day. Dogs like routine and regularity, and it helps them learn not to expect food at odd times of the day. If your dog is a working dog or has a high energy level, you can feed them a bit more after their exercise but still try to keep to a routine as much as possible.

Guidelines for Maintaining a Healthy Weight

Every pet owner wants their dog to be healthy and to have a great quality of life. One of the best ways to do that is to ensure your dog's weight is healthy, but it is important to remember that every dog is different. That means recommendations will vary depending on breed, age, and height. Body conditioning is just as important, and you should seek advice from a veterinarian to ensure your dog is healthy and not under or overweight.

Generally, you should be able to feel your dog's ribs with the minimum amount of fat coverage. You can also look at your dog from above to determine their waist and from the side to see if their stomach slopes up. Their stomach should never hang down.

Keeping your dog's weight healthy is critical to their quality of life. Obesity, or even being a little overweight, can cause serious health problems, including:

- Arthritis
- Cancer
- Diabetes
- Heart disease
- Kidney disease

- Pancreatitis

Ensuring your dog maintains a healthy weight requires you to ensure they eat a balanced diet, get plenty of exercise, and that you take the right preventative steps. Here are some tips to follow:

- **Don't Feed Them Table Scraps:** Common human foods, such as fat trimmings, roast spuds, potato chips, etc., are high-calorie foods, and feeding them to your dog can result in weight gain. Some of them may even be harmful and cause more than just a dodgy tummy.

- **Feed a Balanced Diet:** Your dog must be fed a balanced, nutritious diet, which means every meal provides the right amounts of the right nutrients for each stage of your pet's life. Never use treats as meal substitutes, and never feed more than 10% of their calories in treats.

- **Take Them to the Vet:** Always make sure your dog has regular checkups, where you can ask about weight management and nutrition if needed.

- **Control Portion Sizes:** You must ensure you feed your dog the right service size and not too much or too little. Work out your dog's daily requirements and stick to them – and make sure everyone else in the household does, too.

- **Plenty of Activity:** Keeping your pets active will go a long way towards keeping your dog at a healthy weight. Add some fun activities so your dog enjoys himself, like playing catch, tug-of-war, or heading to the dog park to play with other dogs.

Your dog cannot regulate their meal sizes or nutrition. Only you can do that, so make sure you do the best for your pet and keep them healthy.

Well-Rounded Recipes for Protein-Rich Foods for Overall Health

The rest of this chapter is dedicated to some easy, high-protein recipes you can make for your dog.

Lamb and Carrot Soup

11. Lamb and carrot soup. Source:
https://www.flickr.com/photos/jannon/8466225817/

Ingredients:

- 2 ¾ cups of water
- 5.3 ounces of lamb

- 5.3 ounces of carrot
- 1.7 ounces of pear

Instructions:

1. Rinse the meat and remove any visible fat. Dice the lamb into cubes and cook it over low temperature for about 15 minutes in enough water to cover it.

2. Grate the carrot or dice it into small cubes. Dice the pear into small cubes.

3. Add the carrot and pear to the meat, stir it in, and pour it into a blender or food processor.

4. Process to a smooth, homogenous liquid and let it cool.

5. Pour the mixture into airtight containers and store it in the fridge for no more than three days, or freeze it in portions.

Nutrition Per Serving (3 ½ ounces):

- **Calories**: 51
- **Fat**: 3.1 g
- **Carbs**: 2.1 g
- **Protein**: 3.7 g
- **Fiber**: 0.7 g

Chicken and Green Pea Meatloaf

Ingredients:

- 14 ounces of boneless chicken thighs
- 10.6 ounces of skinless chicken breast

- 1 ounce of liver
- 0.7 ounces of chicken heart
- 1.7 ounces of chicken gizzards
- 7 ounces of green peas

Instructions:

1. Remove any skin from the chicken and cut off any visible fat. Remove bones if there are any, and wash the chicken thoroughly.

2. Clean the offal, soaking it in water for several minutes before removing connective tissues.

3. Preheat your oven to 356°F and grease a loaf pan.

4. Cut the chicken and offal into small cubes and put them through a meat grinder.

5. Add the peas to the ground mixture and stir them in carefully.

6. Press the mixture into the loaf pan and bake for half an hour.

7. Once cooked through, leave the loaf to cool and slice it. Freeze it in portions or refrigerate it in an airtight container – use it within a couple of days.

Nutrition Per Serving (3 ½ ounces):

- **Calories**: 149
- **Fat**: 6.7 g
- **Carbs**: 2.2 g
- **Protein**: 20.8 g
- **Fiber**: 0.6 g

Beef, Tripe, and Sweet Potato

Ingredients:

- 21.2 ounces of lean beef
- 1.7 ounces of beef liver
- 1.7 ounces of beef heart
- 5.3 ounces of green tripe
- 5.3 ounces of sweet potato

Instructions:

1. Cut off any visible fat and remove any bones. Rinse the meat thoroughly.
2. Soak the liver in cold water for several minutes, then remove the connective tissues.
3. Preheat your oven to 356° and prepare a loaf pan.
4. Cut the beef, offal, and tripe into small cubes and put it through a grinder.
5. Cook it in just enough water to cover it.
6. Strain the mixture, cut the potato into small cubes, and stir them into the ground meat.
7. Press the mixture into the loaf pan and bake it for about half an hour.
8. Let it cool, slice it into portions, and refrigerate or freeze it.

Nutrition Per Serving (3 ½ ounces):

- **Calories**: 170
- **Fat**: 7.8 g

- **Carbs**: 3.1 g

- **Protein**: 21.1 g

- **Fiber**: 0.4 g

Chicken, Sweet Potato, and Millet

12. Sweet Potato is a great source of vitamins for dogs. Source: https://www.flickr.com/photos/usdagov/31307598342

Ingredients:

- 14 ounces of chicken thighs

- 5.3 ounces of chicken breast

- 1.2 ounces of chicken liver

- 0.7 ounces of chicken heart

- 1.7 ounces of chicken gizzard

- 5.3 ounces of millet

- 7 ounces of sweet potato

Instructions:

1. Cut half of the fat and skin from the chicken breast and thighs and take any bones out.

2. Soak the offal in cold water for a few minutes, then remove all the connective tissues.

3. Chop the chicken and offal into small cubes, grind it in a meat grinder, and cook it in enough water to cover it.

4. Chop the potatoes into small cubes and stir them in.

5. Cook the millet per the package instructions, then add it to the meat and potatoes – the millet will soak up the liquid. Stir and leave it to cool right down before serving. Store leftovers in the refrigerator or freezer.

Nutrition Per Serving (3 ½ ounces):

- **Calories**: 146
- **Fat**: 5.2 g
- **Carbs**: 5.1 g
- **Protein**: 15.7 g
- **Fiber**: 0.9 g

Beef and Blueberry Kibble

Ingredients:

- 12.3 ounces of oat flour
- 3 ½ ounces of boneless beef
- 2 whole eggs
- 5.3 ounces of beetroot

- 1.7 ounces of blueberries
- 1.1 ounce of coconut oil

Instructions:

1. Preheat your oven to 338°F and place parchment paper over a baking tray.

2. Dice the beetroot into small cubes and combine it with the berries, coconut oil, and eggs.

3. Stir in the oat mixture until combined.

4. Chop the beef into cubes, cook over medium-high heat until cooked through and brown all over, and stir them into the oats.

5. Process the entire mixture in a food processor until it reaches a smooth puree. Add a little water if it is too thick.

6. Spread the mixture evenly over the baking tray in a 5 mm layer.

7. Bake for about 35 to 40 minutes or until dried through and golden brown. Turn the oven down if it looks like it is cooking too quickly.

8. Let it cool, then break it into the size pieces you want.

9. You can store this in an airtight container for up to eight days.

Nutrition Per Serving:

- **Calories**: 269
- **Fat**: 10.5 g
- **Carbs**: 31.6 g
- **Protein**: 12 g

- **Fiber**: 3.4 g

Veggie Protein Power

Ingredients:

- 2 chopped carrots
- 1 peeled and chopped sweet potato
- 1 ½ cups of rinsed green or brown lentils
- 3 ½ cups of water
- 2 lb. of ground chicken or turkey
- 5 ounces of fresh spinach

Instructions:

1. Cook the lentils in the water until they start boiling. Put the lid on, reduce the heat, and simmer until the lentils have absorbed the water.

2. Pulse the sweet potato and carrot in a food processor for a couple of seconds and set them aside.

3. Cook the ground meat in a pan until no longer pink, stirring constantly with a wooden spoon so the meat breaks up.

4. Add the chopped veggies, stir in the spinach, and cook until the veggies are soft, about five minutes. Add a splash of olive oil if you need to.

5. Add the cooked lentils and stir them in.

6. Let the mixture cool, then portion it into food-safe bags or containers, refrigerate for up to seven days, or freeze it for up to three months.

Nutrition Per Serving (1 cup):

- **Calories**: 301
- **Fat**: 3 g
- **Carbs**: 32 g
- **Protein**: 37 g
- **Fiber**: 13 g

Protein Dog Treats

13. Protein dog treats. Source: https://www.pexels.com/photo/dog-food-in-a-glass-container-10880504/

Ingredients:

- 2 ½ cups of whole wheat flour OR oat flour
- ½ cup of warm water
- ¼ up of ground flax
- ½ cup of applesauce – unsweetened OR use pumpkin puree

- 2 tbsp of natural peanut butter
- 2 tbsp of dried parsley
- ½ tsp of ground cinnamon

Instructions:

1. Preheat your oven to 350°F and place parchment paper on a large baking tray.

2. Mix the flax and water and set it aside.

3. After about 10 minutes, place it in a large bowl with the applesauce, parsley, peanut butter, and cinnamon. Mix to combine, then add the flour and mix it into a stiff dough.

4. Scrape the dough out of the bowl onto a floured surface and knead it well. Add a little water if it is too dry.

5. Roll it out about ½-inch thick, then cut it into shapes of your choice or just into squares. Gather the remaining dough up, roll it out, and continue cutting. Repeat until all the dough is gone. This should make 28 treats.

6. Place them on the baking tray in a single layer and bake until dry and golden brown, about 45 to 60 minutes.

7. Let them cool overnight so they dry out thoroughly, then store them in an airtight container. Refrigerate for up to two weeks or freeze.

Nutrition Per Serving (1 treat):

- **Calories**: 53
- **Fat**: 1 g
- **Carbs**: 9 g

- **Protein**: 2 g

- **Fiber**: 2 g

These should get you started, and the next few chapters will give you even more delicious, nutritious recipes for your pup.

Chapter 3: Quick and Nutrient-Rich Meals

When you start moving your dog onto a homemade diet, you want some quick, easy meals packed with nutrients to help your dog transition. All the recipes in this chapter meet those requirements, all easy to prepare in less than two hours and so delicious that your dog will love them. Keep in mind that the serving sizes are relative – it all depends on your dog.

Let's dive in.

Chicken and Pumpkin

14. Chicken and pumpkin. Source:
https://www.flickr.com/photos/avlxyz/49801493401

Prep Time: 10 minutes

Cook Time: 50 minutes

Makes: 8 cups

Ingredients:

- 4 boneless, skinless chicken breasts

- 2 cups of water

- 1 cup of uncooked brown rice

- 1 cup of chopped pumpkin

- 1 tbsp of coconut oil

Instructions:

1. Add the rice and water to a saucepan and bring it to a boil over medium-high heat. Reduce the heat to low, cover the pan and simmer until tender, about half an hour. Turn the heat off and let the rice cool.

2. Put the pumpkin in a pan and add enough water to cover it. Let it come to a boil over medium-high heat, then cover the pan and let it simmer until soft – about 10 minutes.

3. Drain the pumpkin and set it aside.

4. Chop the chicken into chunks. Heat the coconut oil over medium heat and cook the chicken for about eight to ten minutes or until thoroughly cooked.

5. Combine all the ingredients, stirring to make sure they are well distributed and serve.

6. You can store this for up to three days in an airtight container in the fridge or freeze it in Ziploc bags or sealable, freezer-safe containers.

7. If you freeze it, make sure it is thoroughly defrosted and warm it up a little in the microwave before serving.

Nutrition Per Serving (1 cup):

- **Calories**: 234
- **Fat**: 5 g
- **Carbs**: 19 g
- **Protein**: 26 g
- **Fiber**: 1 g

Salmon, Pumpkin, and Spinach

Prep Time: 15 minutes

Cook Time: 25 minutes

Makes: 8 cups

Ingredients:

- 3 lb. of fresh or frozen salmon
- 2 cups of frozen spinach, defrosted
- 1 cup of uncooked brown rice
- 2 cups of water
- 1 cup of frozen peas
- ½ cup of natural pumpkin puree

Instructions:

1. Preheat your oven to 375°F and place parchment paper on a baking tray.

2. Once the oven has reached temperature, place the salmon on the tray and bake it for 20 to 25 minutes.

3. Meanwhile, place the water and rice in a saucepan and bring it to a boil over medium-high heat. Reduce the heat, cover the pan, and simmer the rice for 20 to 25 minutes or until tender.

4. Halfway through cooking, drop the peas into the water and add the spinach towards the end.

5. Drain the rice and peas once cooked and remove the salmon from the oven.

6. Flake the fish using a fork, making sure to remove any bones you find.

7. Mix all the ingredients together and serve.

8. Store in the fridge for up to four days in a sealed container or freeze it in freezer-safe containers or Ziploc bags.

Nutrition Per Serving (1 cup):

- **Calories**: 349
- **Fat**: 12 g
- **Carbs**: 22 g
- **Protein**: 37 g
- **Fiber**: 2 g

Beef and Lamb

Prep Time: 15 minutes

Cook Time: 20 minutes

Makes: 4 servings (8 ounces)

Ingredients:

- 8 ounces of ground lamb
- 8 ounces of lean ground beef
- 2 ounces of chopped beef liver
- 1 ounce of chopped Shiitake mushrooms
- 4 ounces of grated zucchini
- 4 ounces of chopped broccoli
- 3 ounces of chopped green beans
- 2 ounces of cranberries
- 2 tbsp of ground raw pumpkin seeds
- 2 tbsp of ground flaxseed
- 2 tbsp of apple cider vinegar

- 1 tbsp of grated fresh ginger
- 2 tsp of ground turmeric
- 2 tsp of coconut oil
- ½ tsp of sea kelp

Instructions:

1. Heat the coconut oil in a large skillet over medium heat and brown the lamb and beef. Stir it with a wooden spoon to break the meat into smaller bits, then drain off the fat.

2. Add the liver and cook, stirring, for three to four minutes until the liver is fully cooked.

3. Add the berries, veggies, spices, and seeds, give it a good stir and cover the skillet. Simmer until everything is cooked, about 10 to 15 minutes.

4. Take the pan off the heat, let it cool down, and serve.

5. This can be refrigerated for up to three days or frozen for up to three months.

Nutrition Per Serving (8 ounces):

- **Calories**: 375
- **Fat**: 23 g
- **Carbs**: 15 g
- **Protein**: 29 g
- **Fiber**: 4 g

Pork and Veggies

Prep Time: 10 minutes

Cook Time: 20 minutes

Makes: 10 servings (5 ounces each)

Ingredients:

- 2 lb. of lean ground pork
- 4 ounces of beef or pork liver
- 2 ounces of chicken giblets
- 2 whole eggs
- ½ cup of chopped pumpkin
- ½ cup of finely chopped celery
- ½ cup of grated zucchini
- 1 tbsp of chia seeds
- 1 tbsp of hemp hearts
- 1 tbsp of coconut oil
- 1 tsp of grated fresh ginger
- ½ tsp of ground turmeric

Instructions:

1. Heat the coconut oil over medium heat and cook the ground pork until cooked through for about eight to ten minutes.

2. And the giblets and liver and cook for four minutes, or until cooked through.

3. Add the pumpkin, celery, zucchini, chia seeds, hemp hearts, ginger, and turmeric and stir. Crack the eggs in, stir to break them up, and cover the pan. Reduce the heat and cook for about seven to ten minutes until everything is thoroughly cooked.

4. Let it cool before serving. This will keep in the fridge for up to three days, or you can freeze it in portions.

Nutrition Per Serving:

- **Calories**: 305
- **Fat**: 23 g
- **Carbs**: 2 g
- **Protein**: 21g
- **Fiber**: 1 g

Turkey and Rice

15. Turkey and rice. Source: Tiia Monto, CC BY-SA 3.0 <https://creativecommons.org/licenses/by-sa/3.0>, via Wikimedia Commons

Prep Time: 5 minutes

Cook Time: 25 minutes

Makes: 10 cups

Ingredients:

- 1 lb. of lean ground turkey

- 6 cups of water

- 2 cups of uncooked brown rice

- 8 ounces of frozen carrots, cauliflower, and broccoli mix

- 1 tsp of dried rosemary

Instructions:

1. Put the turkey, rice, and water in a large pot, add the rosemary, and stir well to break the turkey up. Heat to a boil over high heat, then reduce it to low and let it simmer for about 20 minutes.

2. Add the veggies, stir, and cook for five minutes, then let the mixture cool.

3. Store in an airtight container in the fridge for up to three days or divide into portions and freeze.

Nutrition Per Serving (1 cup):

- **Calories**: 440

- **Fat**: 10 g

- **Carbs**: 64 g

- **Protein**: 23 g

- **Fiber** 5 g

Turkey and Veggies

Prep Time: 10 minutes

Cook Time: 10 minutes

Makes: 8 servings

Ingredients:

- 2 lb. of ground lean turkey
- 2 tbsp of finely diced chicken liver
- 1 ½ cups of water
- 2 coarsely chopped carrots
- 1 cup of diced green beans
- 1 cup of small cauliflower florets
- 2 tbsp of olive oil

Instructions:

1. Add the water to a saucepan and place a steam basket or metal colander over the top. Place the veggies in the basket, put a lid on, and hat the water until it is boiling. Turn the heat down so the water is at a low boil and steam the veggies for ten minutes or until tender.

2. While the veggies cook, cook the liver and turkey in a large skillet over medium-high heat until cooked through. Drain the fat off.

3. Chop the vegetables finely or put them in a food processor and pulse until chopped. Add them to the turkey, pour in the olive oil, and toss to combine.

4. Let the mixture cool, then serve or freeze in portions.

Nutrition Per Serving:

- **Calories**: 176
- **Fat**: 6 g

- **Carbs**: 3 g
- **Protein**: 28 g
- **Fiber**: 1 g

Turkey Stew

Prep Time: 10 minutes

Cook Time: 25 minutes

Makes: 3 lb.

Ingredients:

- 2 lb. of lean ground turkey
- 4 ounces of beef liver
- 3 ounces of beef kidney
- 6 ounces of sweet potato
- 3 ounces of green beans

Instructions:

1. Peel and chop the sweet potato into small chunks.
2. Trim the beans and chop them into small pieces.
3. Chop the kidney and liver into small pieces.
4. Add the turkey, veggies, kidney, and liver to a large pan, add enough water to cover, and bring to a boil, stirring to break the turkey meat up. Put the lid on, turn the heat down, and simmer until all the meat is cooked through, for about 20 to 25 minutes.
5. Let it cool, then serve it or store it in the refrigerator for a couple of days. You can also freeze it in portions.

Nutrition Per Serving (4 ounces):

- **Calories**: 119
- **Fat**: 2 g
- **Carbs**: 4 g
- **Protein**: 21 g
- **Fiber**: 1 g

Salmon and Vegetable

16. Salmon and vegetables. Source: https://unsplash.com/photos/raw-fish-meat-on-brown-chopping-board-kC9KUtSiflw

Prep Time: 15 minutes

Cook Time: 25 minutes

Makes: 4 cups

Ingredients:

- ½ cup of water
- 2 peeled and diced Russet potatoes (use sweet potatoes if you prefer)
- 1 large peeled and grated carrot
- 1 packed cup of chopped spinach

- 8 ounces of canned or raw salmon
- 1/3 cup of canned pumpkin
- ½ cup of egg whites
- 1 tbsp of coconut oil

Instructions:

1. Heat a heavy skillet over medium heat, then add the water. When it comes to a boil, add the potatoes, put the lid on, and simmer for eight to ten minutes or until soft.

2. Stir in the coconut oil and carrot and cook for two to three minutes. Move the veggies to one side of the skillet and add the egg whites to the empty side. Cook until set, about four to five minutes, then stir them using a wooden spoon to break them up. Stir the egg white pieces in with the potatoes and carrots.

3. Add the salmon and spinach (if using raw salmon, chop it into small pieces first) and stir. Put the lid on and cook for seven to eight minutes until the salmon is cooked through.

4. Add the pumpkin, stir, and take it off the heat. Let it cool before serving.

5. Store leftovers in an airtight container in the fridge or freeze them in portions.

Nutrition Per Serving (1 cup):

- **Calories**: 260
- **Fat**: 11 g
- **Carbs**: 21 g
- **Protein**: 20 g

- **Fiber:** 4 g

Beef and Rice

Prep Time: 15 minutes

Cook Time: 60 minutes

Makes: 18 cups

Instructions:

- 2 lb. of lean ground beef
- 6 cups of water + extra if needed
- 4 cups of uncooked brown rice
- 1 lb. of beef bones – a mixture of marrow, short rib, shank, shin, etc.
- 1 can of carrots, drained (15 ounces)
- 1 can of spinach, drained (13 ½ ounces)
- 1 can of pumpkin puree (15 ounces)
- 6 whole eggs
- 1 tbsp of fresh rosemary, finely chopped

Instructions:

1. Heat a large, heavy pan over medium-high and cook the ground beef, stirring until it is broken down and drowned all over – about five to seven minutes. Drain the excess fat off.

2. Add the rice and water to a soup pot, stir in the beef, rosemary, and bones, and bring it to a boil.

3. Turn the heat down to medium-low and simmer the broth for about 45 minutes. Stir it occasionally and add more water if needed – the rice should be mushy when cooked.

4. While it cooks, put the eggs (whole, with shells) into a blender, add the spinach and carrots, and blend to a smooth puree. Pour it into a bowl, add the pumpkin, and stir to combine.

5. Take the meat off the heat, add the egg mixture, and stir it in. Put it back on the heat and cook for about five minutes, stirring frequently.

6. Let it cool down for about half an hour before serving to your pet.

7. This will keep in the fridge for up to three days or you can freeze it for up to three months.

Nutrition Per Serving (3 cups):

- **Calories**: 846
- **Fat**: 27 g
- **Carbs**: 107 g
- **Protein**: 43 g
- **Fiber**: 9 g

Chapter 4: Puppy-Friendly Delights

Puppies are cute, fluffy bundles, but they require a lot of care, specifically in terms of feeding. And, because they need feeding more often than adult dogs, there is plenty of room for healthy treats, especially helpful when you are training them.

Pup-Friendly Banana Bread

17. Banana bread. Source: https://unsplash.com/photos/baked-bread-DMYcw8JHlgE

Prep Time: 15 minutes

Cook Time: 40 minutes

Makes: 16 slices

Ingredients:

- 1 ½ cups of oat flour
- 1 ripe banana
- 1 whole egg
- ¼ cup of coconut milk
- 1 tsp of ground cinnamon
- ½ tsp of baking powder

Ingredients:

1. Preheat your oven to 325°F and line two mini loaf pans with parchment paper. You can use a large, deep baking dish if you don't have any.

2. Whisk the oat flour, cinnamon, and baking powder in one bowl and mash the banana in another. Add the coconut milk and egg to the banana and stir to combine.

3. Add the dry ingredients and use an electric mixer to combine them thoroughly.

4. Divide the mixture between the loaf pans and bake until a toothpick comes out clean – about 40 to 45 minutes.

5. Turn them onto a wire rack, let them cool down, and slice each into eight. If you used a single baking dish, slice the bread into 16 equal pieces.

6. These can be stored in an airtight container

Nutrition Per Serving (1 piece or slice):

- **Calories**: 63
- **Fat**: 0.4 g
- **Carbs**: 9 g
- **Protein**: 2 g
- **Fiber**:1 g

Pupper Chews

Prep Time: 10 minutes

Cook Time: 3 hours

Makes: 40 chews

Ingredients:

- 2 large sweet potatoes

Instructions:

1. Preheat your oven to 250°F and place parchment paper on two baking trays.

2. Wash, dry, and slice the potatoes into ¼-inch thick coins, approximately 20 from each potato.

3. Spread them on the baking trays and bake for two to three hours. Turn them halfway through cooking.

4. Once they are dry and chewy, let them cool down, then store them in an airtight container in the fridge for up to three weeks.

Nutrition Per Serving (1 chew):

- **Calories**: 10

- **Fat**: 1 g
- **Carbs**: 2 g
- **Protein**: 1 g
- **Fiber**: 1 g

Banana and Peanut Butter Pupcakes

18. Pupcakes! Source: https://unsplash.com/photos/person-holds-tray-of-muffins-on-tray-LqkFX2Km1ao

Prep Time: 15 minutes

Cook Time: 25 minutes

Makes: 12 pupcakes

Ingredients:

- 2 large ripe bananas
- ½ cup of xylitol-free, natural, smooth peanut butter
- 1/3 cup of organic honey
- 2 whole eggs

- 1 ½ cups of All-Purpose or wholewheat flour
- 2 ½ tsp of baking powder
- ¼ cup of olive, canola, peanut, or vegetable oil
- ¾ cup of water

For the Frosting:

- 1 lb. of potatoes
- 2 tbsp of organic honey
- ½ of low-fat, plain yogurt OR sour cream
- 2 to 4 tbsp of water
- 12 small milk bones – for decoration – OPTIONAL

Instructions:

1. Preheat your oven to 350°F and place cupcake liners in a 12-cup muffin pan.

2. Mash the bananas until smooth, and add the honey, eggs, and peanut butter. Whisk to a smooth consistency – use an electric mixer if necessary.

3. Whisk in the flour, oil, baking powder, and water until smooth, then pour it into the 12 cupcake liners.

4. Bake for 22 minutes or until golden on top – a toothpick should come out clean.

5. Let them cool on a wire rack for at least half an hour.

6. Make the frosting. Peel and chop the potatoes into small cubes.

7. Put the potatoes in a pot of water and bring it to a boil over high heat. Cook for about 20 minutes or until the potato is very soft.

8. Drain the potatoes, put them back in the pot, and add the honey, yogurt, and 2 tbsp of water. Use an electric mixer to beat the mixture for a minute at medium speed, then another minute at high speed. Add more water if needed. You want a soft, frosting consistency.

9. Spoon it into a piping bag with a 1 ½ cm round piping nozzle. Pipe onto the pupcakes and add a milk bone to decorate.

10. These can be stored in the fridge in an airtight container for up to a week.

Nutrition Per Serving (1 pupcake):

- **Calories**: 40
- **Fat**: 1 g
- **Carbs**: 8 g
- **Protein**: 1 g
- **Fiber**:1 g

Apple Peanut Butter "Dognuts"

Prep Time: 10 minutes

Cook Time: 10 minutes

Makes: 15

Ingredients:

- 2 cups of whole wheat flour
- ½ cup + 2 tbsp of xylitol-free creamy peanut butter
- 3 tbsp of vegetable oil OR 3 tbsp of melted coconut oil
- 1 cup of unsweetened applesauce

- 2 tbsp of organic honey

- 1 tsp of baking powder

Instructions:

1. Preheat your oven to 350°F and spray nonstick spray over a donut pan.

2. Using a silicon spatula, stir in ½ a cup of peanut butter, the oil, honey, and applesauce in a bowl. The mixture will not look completely smooth.

3. Stir in the baking powder and flour.

4. Transfer the batter to a piping bag or use a large plastic bag with one corner cut off.

5. Pipe the batter, dividing it between 15 donut holes, but don't overfill them.

6. Bake for about ten minutes until golden around the edges and firm to the touch.

7. Transfer the "dognuts" to a plate lined with paper towels and leave them for 10 minutes. You might need to use a skewer to lift them out of the pan.

8. While they cool, put the remaining 2 tbsp of peanut butter into a sturdy sandwich bag and heat it for 20 seconds in the microwave. Cut a small hole in the corner of the bag and drizzle it over the cooled "dognuts," using a back-and-forth motion.

9. These can be stored in an airtight container in the fridge or at room temperature – the peanut butter drizzle will not harden, so things might get a little messy!

Nutrition Per Serving (1 "dognut"):

- **Calories**: 157
- **Fat**: 9 g
- **Carbs**: 18 g
- **Protein**: 5 g
- **Fiber**: 3 g

Blueberry and Banana Puppy Pancakes

Prep Time: 5 minutes

Cook Time: 5 minutes

Makes: 2 pancakes

Ingredients:

- 1 ripe banana
- ¼ cup of oat, almond, soy, or lactose-free milk
- 1 cup whole wheat or oat flour
- 1 cup of blueberries, fresh or frozen-thawed
- 1 tbsp of organic maple syrup
- 2 tsp of baking powder

Instructions:

1. Mash the banana and combine it with the milk into a smooth batter.

2. Add the flour and baking powder and use a fork to combine it until the dry ingredients are just incorporated.

3. Add the blueberries and syrup, stirring to incorporate.

4. Heat a little spray oil in a nonstick pan over medium heat.

5. When hot, add ½ a cup of batter and cook for two to four minutes until browning at the edges. Use a silicon spatula to flip the pancake and cook the other side.

6. Set aside and repeat with the rest of the batter.

Nutrition Per Serving (1 pancake):

- **Calories**: 824
- **Fat**: 6 g
- **Carbs**: 172 g
- **Protein**: 28 g
- **Fiber**: 21 g

Bacon and Cheddar Delights

Prep Time: 15 minutes

Cook Time: 20 minutes

Makes: 15

Ingredients:

- 2/3 cup of diced bacon
- 1 cup of rolled oats
- ½ cup of shredded cheddar
- ½ cup of whole wheat flour
- 2 whole eggs

Instructions:

1. Preheat your oven to 350°F and place parchment paper on a baking tray.

2. Combine all the ingredients in one bowl, using clean hands to form it into a well-mixed dough.

3. Flour a board lightly, or use finely ground oats, and roll the dough out thinly.

4. Use cookie cutters to cut your shapes or form the dough into a square and cut it into 15 equal pieces.

5. Place the shapes on the prepped tray and bake for about 25 minutes until golden brown.

6. Allow them to cool and store in an airtight container.

Nutrition Per Serving (1 biscuit):

- **Calories**: 76
- **Fat**: 4.8 g
- **Carbs**: 4.8 g
- **Protein**: 3.3 g
- **Fiber**: 0.68 g

Fish and Veggie Omelet

Prep Time: 15 minutes

Cook Time: 5 minutes

Makes: 1 ½ cups

Ingredients:

- 2 whole eggs

- ¼ cup of diced bell pepper
- ½ cup of canned salmon
- 1 tsp of olive oil

Instructions:

1. Heat the oil over medium heat and scramble the eggs.
2. Add the peppers and salmon, stir to break the fish into smaller bits, and continue scrambling.
3. Cook for about five minutes, stirring frequently, and then take it off the heat.
4. Let it cool before feeding your dog.

Nutrition Per Serving (1/2 cup):

- **Calories**: 98
- **Fat**: 6.2 g
- **Carbs**: 1 g
- **Protein**: 9.4 g
- **Fiber**: 0.1 g

Pumpkin Muffins

Prep Time: 15 minutes

Cook Time: 15 minutes

Makes: 24 minis

Ingredients:

- 3 cups of oat flour
- 2 eggs

- 1 cup of unsweetened applesauce
- 1 tbsp of baking soda
- ¼ cup of melted coconut oil
- ½ cup of pumpkin puree*

Instructions:

1. Preheat your oven to 350°F and use coconut oil to grease two 12-cup mini muffin pans or one 24-cup pan.
2. Whisk the baking soda and flour, then stir in the eggs, pumpkin, applesauce, and coconut oil until just combined.
3. Transfer the batter to the muffin cups, filling each one 2/3 full.
4. Bake until a toothpick or skewer comes out clean, about 15 to 20 minutes.
5. Let them cool for a few minutes, then turn them out onto a wire rack to cool right down.
6. Store in an airtight container

* Do not substitute for pumpkin pie filling, as this is made with spices that can harm your dog.

Nutrition Per Serving (1 mini muffin):

- **Calories**: 91
- **Fat**: 4 g
- **Carbs**: 11 g
- **Protein**: 3 g
- **Fiber**: 1 g

Chicken and Oatmeal Pâté

Prep Time: 20 minutes

Cook Time: 40 minutes

Makes: 40 small servings

Ingredients:

- 1 ½ lb. of skinless, boneless chicken breast
- 1 cup of oatmeal
- ¼ cup of diced carrots
- ¼ cup of peas
- ¼ cup of natural, smooth peanut butter
- 2 tbsp of chia seeds

Instructions:

1. Preheat your oven to 350°F and grease a standard loaf tin.

2. Cook the oatmeal per the instructions on the packet, and then leave it to cool down.

3. Add the chicken to a stock pot, cover with water and bring to a boil. Boil until cooked all the way through, then drain and shred the chicken.

4. While the chicken is cooking, steam the peas and carrots. You can do this in the microwave, using a steamer, or a double boiler.

5. Combine all the ingredients in a large bowl, stirring to bring everything together.

6. Press into the loaf pan, smooth it over, and bake it for 40 minutes.

7. Let the pâté cool down completely before slicing it into small pieces.

8. Store it for up to five days in the fridge in an airtight container or freeze it for up the three months.

This is perfect for dogs with dental problems and those with sensitive stomachs and it can be gently warmed through before serving.

Nutrition Per Serving:

- **Calories**: 200

- **Fat**: 9 g

- **Carbs**: 15 g

- **Protein**: 15 g

- **Fiber**: 4 g

Carrot and Cheddar Chewies

Prep Time: 10 minutes

Cook Time: 12 minutes

Makes: 60

Ingredients:

- 2 cups of whole wheat flour

- 1 cup of old-fashioned oatmeal

- ½ cup of finely grated carrot

- ½ cup of unsweetened, plain Greek yogurt

- ½ cup of shredded cheddar

- 1/3 cup of broth – must be dog-safe (no garlic, onion, etc.) OR water

- 1 egg

- 2 tsp of baking powder

Instructions:

1. Preheat your oven to 325°F and prepare two baking trays – spray with cooking spray or use parchment paper.

2. Whisk the baking powder and flour in a bowl.

3. Put the yogurt, cheese, carrot, oatmeal, and half of the flour in a stand mixer bowl and mix on low speed, gradually adding the remaining flour, alternatively, use a bowl and electric hand mixer.

4. Beat the egg lightly, drizzle it into the mixer with the broth or water, and turn the speed to medium. Continue mixing until all the ingredients are combined.

5. Form a ball from a tsp of mixture, place it on the baking sheet, and repeat with the rest of the mixture.

6. Bake for 12 minutes, until soft in the middle but golden on the outside.

7. Let them cool down and freeze or refrigerate in a sealed container for up to three days.

Nutrition Per Serving (1 chewie):

- **Calories**: 23

- **Fat**: 1 g

- **Carbs**: 4 g

- **Protein**: 1 g
- **Fiber**: 1 g

Oat Cinnamon Apple Dog Treats

Prep Time: 10 minutes

Cook Time: 15 minutes

Makes: 26 small cookies

Ingredients:

- 3 cups of oats
- 2 apples
- 2 tbsp of organic honey
- 1 tbsp of flaxseed
- 2 tsp of ground cinnamon

Instructions:

1. Preheat your oven to 350°F and line a baking tray with parchment paper or a silicone baking mat.

2. Use a food processor to grind 2 cups of oats into a very fine consistency, then transfer them to a large bowl.

3. Core the apples, remove all seeds, and chop the flesh roughly. Run it through the food processor until it is similar to apple sauce, scraping the sides down. A few small chunks are okay.

4. Add the mixture to the oats, then add the whole oats, flaxseed, cinnamon, and honey. Stir to combine. If it is too wet, add more oats; if it is too dry, add a little water or honey.

---

5. Dust a clean surface lightly with flour and roll the dough out to about ¼-inch thick. Cut out cookie shapes and lay them on the prepped tray.

6. Bake for 15 minutes, then turn the oven off. Leave the cookies in the oven for two hours, until crunchy. If your dog prefers softer treats, remove them after 15 minutes and let them cool down at room temperature.

7. Store for up to two weeks in the fridge in a sealed container if the cookies are soft. They can be stored at room temperature if you let them go crunchy and hard.

Nutrition Per Serving (1 small cookie):

- **Calories**: 50
- **Fat**: 1 g
- **Carbs**: 10 g
- **Protein**: 1 g
- **Fiber**: 1 g

Blueberry Frozen Dog Treats

19. Blueberries are healthy fruit that are great for dogs. Source: https://unsplash.com/photos/blueberries-on-white-ceramic-container-4qujjbj3srs

Prep Time: 5 minutes

Cook Time: 0 minutes

Makes: 8

Ingredients:

- ¾ cup of blueberries
- ¾ cup of plain Greek yogurt
- ½ a ripe banana

Instructions:

1. Place all the ingredients in a food processor and blend for about 90 seconds until fully mixed.

2. Pour the mixture into an ice cube tray or silicon puppy treat mold and freeze for up to two hours until frozen solid.

3. Store in an airtight container or Ziploc bag in the freezer and use within three months.

Nutrition Per Serving (1 treat):

- **Calories**: 26
- **Fat**: 1 g
- **Carb**: 4 g
- **Protein**: 2 g
- **Fiber**: 1 g

Chicken and Brown Rice Bowl

Prep Time: 10 minutes

Cook Time: 30 minutes

Makes: 1

Ingredients:

- ½ lb. of chicken breast
- ½ cup of uncooked brown rice
- 1 cup of water
- ¼ cup of diced carrots
- ¼ cup of peas
- 2 tbsp of natural creamy peanut butter
- 1 egg

Instructions:

1. Cook the rice in the water per the packet instructions.

2. Hard-boil the egg and steam the veggies. Dice the chicken breast and cook it over medium high heat until cooked through.

3. Drain the rice, peel and chop the egg, and combine all the ingredients in one bowl, stirring to combine everything.

4. Cool to room temperature before serving. If you are making this ahead of time, you can store this for up to three days in the fridge.

Nutrition Per Serving:

- **Calories**: 210
- **Fat**: 8 g
- **Carbs**: 18 g
- **Protein**: 22 g
- **Fiber**: 2 g

Pork and Apple Casserole

Prep Time: 15 minutes

Cook Time: 45 minutes

Makes: 1

Ingredients:

- ½ lb. of pork loin
- 1 cup of diced apples
- ¼ cup of diced sweet potato
- ¼ cup of trimmed, chopped green beans

- ½ cup of dog-safe chicken broth
- 2 tbsp of buckwheat flour

Instructions:

1. Preheat the oven to 350°F.
2. Dice and cook the pork over medium-high heat until cooked through.
3. Cook the diced sweet potato – you can do this in the microwave in just a few minutes.
4. Combine all the ingredients in one bowl, add the broth last, then transfer it to a casserole dish.
5. Bake until it is bubbling hot and starting to go brown on top, about 45 minutes.
6. Remove it from the oven and let the casserole cool right down.
7. This will keep in the fridge for up to three days or you can freeze it for up to three months.

Nutrition Per Serving:

- **Calories**: 240
- **Fat**: 8 g
- **Carbs**: 20 g
- **Protein**: 20 g
- **Fiber**: 3 g

Tuna and Brown Rice Surprise

20. Tuna and brown rice. Source:
https://www.pexels.com/photo/white-rice-on-red-bowl-5604827/

Prep Time: 10 minutes

Cook Time: 15 minutes

Makes: 3 cups

Ingredients:

- 1 cup of tuna canned in water, drained
- ½ cup of uncooked brown rice
- 1 cup of water
- ½ cup of trimmed, chopped green beans
- ¼ cup of cubed carrots
- ¼ cup of peas
- 1 tbsp of cooking oil

Instructions:

1. Add the rice and water to a pot and cook per the package instructions.

2. Meanwhile, cook the beans and carrots in boiling water and steam the peas until soft.

3. Drain the rice and veggies and mash the peas.

4. Blend all the ingredients in one bowl, mixing until thoroughly combined.

5. Refrigerate in a sealed container for up to three days.

Nutrition Per Serving (1 cup):

- **Calories**: 250
- **Fat**: 7 g
- **Carbs**: 29 g
- **Protein**: 16 g
- **Fiber**: 2 g

Poultry and Carrot Casserole

Prep Time: 15 minutes

Cook Time: 40 minutes

Makes: 6 cups

Ingredients:

- 1 lb. of ground chicken or turkey
- 1 cup of white rice
- 1 cup of chopped carrots
- 1 cup of trimmed green beans

- 1 liter of water
- 2 tbsp of olive oil

Instructions:

1. Heat the olive oil over medium heat in a large stock pot.

2. Cook the ground meat until cooked through and browned, stirring with a wooden spoon to break it up.

3. Add the rice, beans, and carrots, stir, and add the water.

4. Bring it to a boil, then turn the heat down, cover, and simmer for about half an hour. When the veggies are soft and the rice cooked, it is done – stir occasionally so it doesn't burn.

5. Let it cool down before storing or serving. This can be stored for up to three days in the fridge.

Nutrition Per Serving (1 cup):

- **Calories**: 315
- **Fat**: 10 g
- **Carbs**: 37 g
- **Protein**: 28 g
- **Fiber**: 1 g

Salmon and Potato Mash

Prep Time: 10 minutes

Cook Time: 20 minutes

Makes: 2 cups

Ingredients:

- 1 cup of canned salmon
- 1 cup of sweet potato cubes
- ½ cup of peas
- ¼ cup of cubed carrots
- ¼ cup of plain Greek yogurt
- 1 tbsp of olive oil

Instructions:

1. Cook and mash the potatoes and peas separately.
2. Cook the carrots.
3. Combine all the ingredients in one bowl, stirring until everything is thoroughly mixed.
4. This can be stored in the fridge for up to three days in an airtight container.

Nutrition Per Serving (1 cup):

- **Calories**: 280
- **Fat**: 9 g
- **Carbs**: 25 g
- **Protein**: 20 g
- **Fiber**: 1 g

Chapter 5: Wholesome Recipes for Older Dogs

While older dogs can be fed roughly the same diet as their younger counterparts, there may be times or situations when they need different food. For example, if they are not so active, they don't need so many carbs in their food, as they won't be burning off. Or they may need to go on a lower fat or lower calorie diet. This chapter offers a selection of wholesome recipes to keep your senior dog healthy and happy.

21. Older dogs have different diet requirements to stay healthy. Source: https://www.pexels.com/photo/brown-dog-eating-8434676/

Beef and Sweet Potato Stew

Prep Time: 15 minutes

Cook Time: 30 minutes

Makes: 6 cups

Ingredients:

- 1 lb. of lean ground beef
- 2 peeled and cubed sweet potatoes
- 1 cup of frozen peas
- 1 cup of chopped carrots
- 1 liter of water
- 2 tbsp of olive oil

Instructions:

1. Heat the olive oil in a large pot over medium heat.
2. Cook the ground beef until browned all over, breaking it into smaller pieces by stirring.
3. Add the potato cubes, carrots, and peas, stir to combine, then add the water.
4. Bring the stew to a boil, reduce the heat, put a lid on, and simmer for 20 to 25 minutes until the veggies and potato are soft.
5. Turn off the heat, let the stew cool, then serve.
6. This can be stored in the fridge for up to three days or frozen for up to three months.

Nutrition Per Serving (1 cup):

- **Calories**: 308

- **Fat**: 18 g
- **Carbs**: 13g
- **Protein**: 22 g
- **Fiber**: 1 g

Tilapia and Quinoa Mix

Prep Time: 10 minutes

Cook Time: 20 minutes

Makes: 2 cups

Ingredients:

- 1 cup of tilapia
- ½ cup of uncooked quinoa
- 2 cups of water
- 1 cup of sweet potato cubes
- ¼ cup of trimmed, chopped green beans
- ¼ cup of cranberries

Instructions:

1. Cook the tilapia, let it cool, and flake it with a fork.
2. Cook the sweet potatoes and mash them.
3. Cook the quinoa per the package instructions.
4. Cook the beans and carrots.
5. Combine everything in a bowl and serve warm.
6. Store in an airtight container in the fridge for up to three days.

Nutrition Per Serving (1 cup):

- **Calories**: 250
- **Fat**: 1.5 g
- **Carbs**: 50 g
- **Protein**: 15 g
- **Fiber**: 2 g

Salmon and Sweet Potato Delight

Prep Time: 10 minutes

Cook Time: 30 minutes

Makes: 1

Ingredients:

- ½ lb. of salmon
- 2 cups of sweet potato cubes
- ¼ cup of peas
- ¼ cup of finely chopped carrots
- 2 tbsp of oat flour
- 1 tbsp of olive oil
- 2 tbsp of low-fat cottage cheese

Instructions:

1. Heat your oven to 350°F and grease an oven-proof baking dish.

2. Cook the salmon, potato, and veggies. Mash the potato, flake the salmon, and combine everything except the cottage cheese in one bowl.

3. Transfer it to the baking dish, press it down, and spread cottage cheese over the top.

4. Bake it until the edges are golden brown, about half an hour.

5. Allow it to cool before you feed your dog.

6. This will last in the fridge for up to four days and in the freezer for up to a month.

Nutrition Per Serving:

- **Calories**: 250
- **Fat**: 10 g
- **Carbs**: 18 g
- **Protein**: 22 g
- **Fiber**: 3 g

Lamb and Vegetable Delight

Prep Time: 15 minutes

Cook Time: 40 minutes

Makes: 5 cups

Ingredients:

- 1 lb. of ground lamb
- 1 cup of white rice
- 1 cup of peas

- 4 cups of cubed zucchini
- 1 liter of water
- 2 tbsp of canola oil

Instructions:

1. Heat the oil in a soup pot over medium heat and cook the lamb, stirring to break it up and brown it all over.

2. Add the rice, zucchini, and peas, stir it together, then add the water.

3. When the mixture comes to a boil, turn the heat down, cover the pot, and simmer until the veggies and rice are cooked, about half an hour.

4. Leave it to cool down before serving to your dog.

5. Refrigerate leftovers for up to three days.

Nutrition Per Serving (1 cup):

- **Calories**: 375
- **Fat**: 11 g
- **Carbs**: 40 g
- **Protein**: 23 g
- **Fiber**: 2 g

Chicken, Sweet Potato and Millet

Prep Time: 10 minutes

Cook Time: 20 minutes

Makes: 10 servings

Ingredients:

- 14 ounces of chicken thighs
- 5.3 ounces of chicken breast
- 1.1 ounces of chicken liver
- 0.7 ounce of chicken heart
- 1.7 ounces of chicken gizzards
- 5.3 ounces of millet
- 7 ounces of sweet potato

Instructions:

1. Cut off half the visible fat and skin from the thighs and remove any bones. Rinse the thighs.

2. Soak the gizzard, heart, and liver for a few minutes and cut out the connective tissues.

3. Slice the meat and offal into small cubes and grind them coarsely.

4. Place the ground meat and offal in a saucepan and add enough water to cover it. Heat over medium heat.

5. Cut the sweet potato into small cubes and add it to the pan. While the mixture is cooking, cook the millet in a separate pan per the package directions. Add it to the simmering meat and potatoes, stir, and let it simmer until most of the liquid is absorbed.

6. Let it cool down before serving.

7. You can refrigerate this for up to three days or freeze in portions for up to three months.

Nutrition Per Serving (3 ½ ounces):

- **Calories**: 146
- **Fat**: 5.2 g
- **Carbs**: 5.1 g
- **Protein**: 15.7 g
- **Fiber**: 0.9 g

Beef, Turkey Breast, and Barley

Prep Time: 10 minutes

Cook Time: 20 minutes

Makes: 10 servings

Ingredients:

- 14 ounces of lean beef
- 5.3 ounces of lean turkey breast
- 1.7 ounces of beef liver
- 1.8 ounces of beef heart
- 5.3 ounces of barley
- 7 ounces of bell pepper
- 1 egg

Instructions:

1. Rinse the beef and cut it into cubes.
2. Soak the liver and heart for a few minutes, then cut out the connective tissues. Cut it into cubes. Feed the beef and offal cubes through a meat grinder and put them

in a pan with just enough water to cover them. Heat over medium heat.

3. Cut the bell pepper into cubes and stir it into the mixture.

4. Cook the barley per the package directions and then add it to the simmering mixture.

5. Cook until the liquid is almost absorbed, then turn off the heat and let it cool down.

6. Refrigerate for no more than three days or freeze for no more than three months.

Nutrition Per Serving (3 ½ ounces):

- **Calories**: 164
- **Fat**: 6.2 g
- **Carbs**: 7.3 g
- **Protein**: 19.6 g
- **Fiber**:1.2 g

Beef, Cod, and White Rice

Prep Time: 10 minutes

Cook Time: 20 minutes

Makes: 10 servings

Ingredients:

- 14 ounces of lean beef
- 5.3 ounces of cod fillet
- 1.7 ounces of beef liver

- 1.8 ounces of beef heart
- 5.3 ounces of white rice
- 7 ounces of beetroot
- 1 egg

Instructions:

1. Rinse the beef and chop it into cubes. Clean the offal, cut the connective tissues out and cut it all into cubes. Run everything through a grinder.
2. Put it all in a saucepan, cover with water, and heat over medium heat.
3. Cut the cod into small pieces and add it to the mixture.
4. Cut the bet into small cubes, stir them into the mixture, and add the egg.
5. Cook the rice per the package directions, then stir it in and leave it to heat until the water is almost gone, stirring occasionally.
6. Serv when it has cooled.
7. Store in the refrigerator for up to three days and the freezer for a month.

Nutrition Per Serving (3 ½ ounces):

- **Calories**: 161
- **Fat**: 6.2 g
- **Carbs**: 6.3 g
- **Protein**: 18.6 g
- **Fiber**:1.2 g

Duck and Pear Ragout

Prep Time: 20 minutes

Cook Time: 45 minutes

Makes: 1

Ingredients:

- ½ lb. of cooked duck breast, shredded
- 1 cup of diced pears
- ¼ cup of diced sweet potato
- ¼ cup of chopped green beans
- 2 tbsp of oatmeal
- ¼ cup of blueberries
- 1 tbsp of honey

Instructions:

1. Cook the sweet potato in the microwave until soft, about 5 minutes. Mix the oatmeal with hot water to cook it.

2. Combine the duck, potato, beans, pears, and oatmeal in a saucepan. Add enough water to cover it and heat to a simmer over medium heat.

3. When it is simmering, reduce the heat, cover the pan, and let it cook for half an hour, stirring a few times.

4. Add the blueberries and honey, stir, and heat for 10 minutes.

5. Let it cool to room temperature before serving.

6. Store in the fridge for up to three days or the freezer for up to three months.

Nutrition Per Serving:

- **Calories**: 310
- **Fat**: 12 g
- **Carbs**: 25 g
- **Protein**: 22 g
- **Fiber**:4 g

Beef and Barley Bowl

22. Beef and barley bowl. Source:
https://www.flickr.com/photos/jeffreyww/38958814481

Prep Time: 20 minutes

Cook Time: 40 minutes

Makes: 1

Ingredients:

- ½ lb. of lean ground beef
- 1 cup of barley
- ¼ cup of diced zucchini
- ¼ cup of chopped spinach
- 2 tbsp of oat flour
- ¼ cup of diced pumpkin
- 1 tbsp of flaxseed oil

Instructions:

1. Cook the pumpkin in the microwave until soft, then mash it and set aside.
2. Cook the barley per the package directions.
3. Heat a large skillet over medium heat, cook the beef until browned, then drain the fat.
4. Add the barley, mashed pumpkin, zucchini, oat flour, and spinach, and stir to combine.
5. Turn the heat to low and cook for 10 minutes until heated through, stirring now and then.
6. Allow it to cool down before serving, and store leftovers in the fridge for up to three days in an airtight container. Alternatively, freeze it for up to three months.

Nutrition Per Serving:

- **Calories**: 300
- **Fat**: 10 g
- **Carbs**: 30 g

- **Protein**: 22 g
- **Fiber**: 6 g

Pork and Butternut Squash Pudding

Prep Time: 15 minutes

Cook Time: 30 minutes

Makes: 1

Ingredients:

- ½ lb. of cooked, shredded pork
- 1 cup of cubed butternut squash
- ¼ cup of finely chopped parsnip
- ¼ cup of cranberries
- ¼ cup of trimmed, chopped green beans
- 2 tbsp of gluten-free flour

Instructions:

1. Preheat your oven to 375°F and spray a small oven-proof dish with a little oil.
2. Cook the butternut in the microwave, then mash it.
3. Combine the shredded pork with the mashed squash, green beans, cranberries, flour, and parsnip, stirring to thoroughly combine.
4. Transfer it to the prepared dish and smooth it over.
5. Bake until golden and firm, about half an hour.

6. Let it cool before serving or storing. This can be refrigerated for up to three days or frozen for up to three months.

Nutrition Per Serving:

- **Calories**: 280
- **Fat**: 10 g
- **Carbs**: 25 g
- **Protein**: 22 g
- **Fiber**: 5 g

Cod, Salmon, and Buckwheat

Prep Time: 10 minutes

Cook Time: 20 minutes

Makes: 10 servings

Ingredients:

- 14 ounces of cod fillet
- 10.6 ounces of boneless salmon
- 1.7 ounces of venison liver
- 1.8 ounces of venison heart
- 3 ½ ounces of buckwheat
- 3 ½ ounces of small-diced pumpkin

Instructions:

1. Soak the offal in cold water for a few minutes, then slice off all connective tissues.

2. Chop the cod, salmon, and offal into small cubes and grind them through a meat grinder.

3. Place the meat in a pan, cover it with water, and heat over medium heat.

4. Cook the buckwheat per the directions on the package, then drain it and add it to the meat.

5. Add the pumpkin, stir it in, and heat until the pumpkin is cooked.

6. Let it cool before serving. This can be stored in the fridge for up to three days or in the freezer.

Nutrition Per Serving (3 ½ ounces):

- **Calories**: 128
- **Fat**: 2.2 g
- **Carbs**: 6.1 g
- **Protein**: 18.3 g
- **Fiber**: 0.8g

Venison, Lamb, and Brown Rice

Prep Time: 10 minutes

Cook Time: 20 minutes

Makes: 10 servings

Ingredients:

- 14 ounces of venison
- 10.6 ounces of lamb
- 1.7 ounces of venison liver

- 1.8 ounces of venison heart
- 3 ½ ounces of brown rice, soaked
- 3 ½ ounces of cubed pumpkin

Instructions:

1. Cook the rice per the directions on the packet.
2. Rinse the meat and remove the connective tissues from the offal.
3. Chop the lamb, venison, and offal into small cubes and put it through a meat grinder.
4. Place the meat in a saucepan with enough water to cover it and heat it over medium heat.
5. Add the cooked rice and pumpkins, stir it all together, and heat until cooked through and the liquid has been absorbed.
6. Cool it, then serve or store it in the fridge for up to three days.

Nutrition Per Serving (3 ½ ounces):

- **Calories**: 131
- **Fat**: 2.3 g
- **Carbs**:6.3 g
- **Protein**: 22.7 g
- **Fiber**: 0.8 g

Turkey Breast, Rabbit and White Rice

Prep Time: 10 minutes

Cook Time: 30 minutes

Makes: 10 servings

Ingredients:

- 14 ounces of turkey breast
- 10.6 ounces of rabbit
- 1.7 ounces of venison liver
- 10.8 ounces of venison heart
- 3 ½ ounces of white rice
- 3 ½ ounces of broccoli

Instructions:

1. Cook the rice and drain it.
2. Clean the offal and chop it into cubes.
3. Cube the meat and run it through the grinder with the offal.
4. Heat in a pan over medium heat with enough water to cover it. Chop the broccoli and add it to the pan.
5. Stir the rice in and cook until the broccoli is soft and the water has been absorbed.
6. Cool and serve, or store in the refrigerator for up to three days.

Nutrition Per Serving (3 ½ ounces):

- **Calories**: 124
- **Fat**: 2.1 g
- **Carbs**: 6.7 g
- **Protein**: 19.2 g

- **Fiber**: 0.6 g

Cheesy Apple Bites

Prep Time: 10 minutes

Cook Time: 15 minutes

Makes: 20

Ingredients:

- 2 apples
- 1 cup of oat flour
- ½ cup low-fat cheese
- ¼ cup of water
- 1 egg

Instructions:

1. Preheat your oven to 350°F and put baking paper on a baking sheet.
2. Peel and grate the apple, beat the egg, and grate the cheese.
3. Mix all the ingredients together in one bowl, stirring to form a dough.
4. Divide the mixture into 20 small pieces and place them on the sheet.
5. Bake for about 15 minutes or until they start to turn golden brown.
6. Let them cool and store in the fridge for up to two weeks in an airtight container.

Nutrition Per Serving (1 treat):

- **Calories**: 30
- **Fat**: 1 g
- **Carbs**: 5 g
- **Protein**: 1 g
- **Fiber**: 1 g

Chapter 6: Grain-Free and Hypoallergenic Food for Dogs with Allergies

Like humans, dogs can suffer from allergies, resulting in itchy skin, upset stomachs, and bad diarrhea. If your dog is confirmed to have an allergy, you should think about changing his diet, and the recipes in this chapter are all suitable.

Turkey and Carrot

Prep Time: 10 minutes

Cook Time: 25 minutes

Makes: 5

Ingredients:

- ¾ lb. of cooked, shredded turkey breast
- ¼ cup of diced carrots
- ¼ cup of blueberries
- 1 tbsp of almond flour

Instructions:

1. Steam the carrots to soften them.

2. Put all the ingredients into one bowl and stir to combine thoroughly. If you want a little extra flavor, lightly mash the blueberries before mixing them in.

3. Serve at room temperature.

4. Store in the fridge for up to three days.

Nutrition Per Serving (1/5 of the recipe):

- **Calories**: 210

- **Fat**: 6 g

- **Carbs**: 9 g

- **Protein**: 31 g

- **Fiber:** 2 g

Crab and Chickpea Fusion

23. Crab and chickpea. Source: E4024, CC BY-SA 4.0 <https://creativecommons.org/licenses/by-sa/4.0>, via Wikimedia Commons.
https://commons.wikimedia.org/wiki/File:Nohut_yahnisi_(etsiz).j pg

---

Prep Time: 15 minutes

Cook Time: 10 minutes

Makes: 10 servings

Ingredients:

- ½ lb. of cooked crab meat
- 1 cup of cooked chickpeas
- ¼ cup of chopped spinach
- ¼ cup of diced cucumber
- 2 tbsp of plain unsweetened yogurt
- 1 tbsp of chia seeds

Instructions:

1. Mash the chickpeas.
2. Combine all the ingredients in a bowl, stirring gently to combine.
3. Serve at room temperature or cold.
4. This can be stored in the fridge for up to three days.

Nutrition Per Serving:

- **Calories**: 230
- **Fat**: 6 g
- **Carbs**: 20 g
- **Protein**: 24 g
- **Fiber:** 5 g

Vegetarian Broth

Prep Time: 10 minutes

Cook Time: 60 to 90 minutes

Makes: 6 cups

Ingredients:

- 4 cups of water
- 1 peel and diced large sweet potato
- 1 cup of trimmed, chopped green beans
- ¼ cup of blueberries
- 1 tsp of ground flaxseed

Instructions:

1. Pour the water into a pan and add the potato, blueberries, and beans. Bring them to a boil over medium-high heat, then reduce the heat.

2. Cover the pot and simmer for 60 to 90 minutes until all the veggies are tender.

3. Allow the mixture to cool fully, then use an immersion blender to puree it to a smooth consistency.

4. Add the flaxseed and stir it through.

5. If it is too thick, add a little extra water.

6. Serve cold or at room temperature.

7. This can be frozen for up to three months or stored in the fridge for up to five days.

Nutrition Per Serving (1 cup):

- **Calories**: 35

- **Fat**: 0.5 g
- **Carbs**: 8 g
- **Protein**: 1 g
- **Fiber:** 2 g

Salmon and Spinach Combo

Prep Time: 5 minutes

Cook Time: 15 minutes

Makes: 4

Ingredients:

- ¾ lb. of skinless salmon fillet
- ¼ cup of chopped spinach
- ¼ cup of cubed sweet potato
- 1 tbsp of flaxseeds

Instructions:

1. Place the salmon in a pan with a little water and a pinch of salt. Poach the fish, let it cool right down, and then flake it with a fork.

2. Meanwhile, cook the potato and mash it.

3. Put the spinach in the salmon water and wilt it for a minute or two.

4. Combine all the ingredients in one bowl, stirring gently.

5. Serve at room temperature or cool – stir in a little water if your dog needs a softer food.

6. This can be stored in the fridge for up to three days.

Nutrition Per Serving (1/4 of the recipe):

- **Calories**: 230
- **Fat:** 7 g
- **Carbs**: 10 g
- **Protein**: 34 g
- **Fiber:** 2 g

Chicken and Vegetable Broth

24. Chicken and vegetable broth. Source: https://unsplash.com/photos/stainless-steel-cooking-pot-with-white-and-green-soup-IPwNSeSYLJc

Prep Time: 15 minutes

Cook Time: 2 to 2 ½ hours

Makes: 6 cups

Ingredients:

- 1 lb. of skinless, boneless chicken thighs or breast

- 4 cups of water
- 2 peeled, chopped carrots
- 1 chopped celery stalk
- 1 peeled, cubed small sweet potato
- ½ tsp of ground turmeric
- 1 tbsp of finely chopped fresh parsley

Instructions:

1. Put the chicken in a large stock pot, add the potato, celery, and carrots, and pour in the water.

2. Stir the turmeric in and turn the heat to medium-high. Bring the broth to a vegetable, then reduce the heat, put a lid on, and simmer it for two to two and half hours until the chicken is cooked and the veggies are soft. The liquid should be a rich deep color.

3. Once the broth has cooled, gently lift the chicken out and shred it. Add it back to the broth, add the parsley, and stir it.

4. Serve poured onto dry food or as a complete meal for dogs with dental issues or who need extra hydration. Store it in the refrigerator.

Nutrition Per Serving (1 cup):

- **Calories**: 40
- **Fat**: 1 g
- **Carbs**: 3 g
- **Protein**: 5 g
- **Fiber:** 1 g

Venison and Cranberry Stew

Prep Time: 20 minutes

Cook Time: 50 minutes

Makes: 1

Ingredients:

- ½ lb. of cooked, shredded venison
- 1 cup of fresh or frozen cranberries
- ¼ cup of cooked lentils
- ¼ cup of diced carrots
- ½ cup of water
- 2 tbsp of almond flour
- 1 tbsp of organic maple syrup

Instructions:

1. Put all the ingredients, except the maple syrup, in a large stop pot and add enough water to cover it. Bring it to a boil over medium-high heat, then turn it down, put a lid on, and simmer it for 50 minutes. Stir occasionally.

2. Stir the syrup in, heat for 10 minutes, then let it cool.

3. Store in the fridge for no more than three days or the freezer for up to three months.

Nutrition Per Serving:

- **Calories**: 280
- **Fat**: 10 g
- **Carbs**: 20 g

- **Protein**: 26 g
- **Fiber**: 5 g

Herring and Pumpkin

Prep Time: 15 minutes

Cook Time: 30 minutes

Makes: 1

Ingredients:

- ½ lb. of cooked, flaked herring
- 1 cup of pumpkin cubes
- ¼ cup of peas
- ¼ cup of diced carrots
- ½ cup of water
- 2 tbsp of gluten-free flour
- 1 tbsp of coconut oil

Instructions:

1. Heat the coconut oil in a soup pot over medium heat.
2. Cook the carrots and peas until slightly soft.
3. Meanwhile, microwave the pumpkin until soft, then mash it.
4. Add the flour to the peas and carrots, stir it in, then gradually add the water, continuing to stir until fully combined.
5. Add the herring and pumpkin, turn the heat down, and simmer it for about 25 minutes.

6. Allow it to cool before serving.

7. Store in the refrigerator for up to four days or the freezer for up to a month.

Nutrition Per Serving:

- **Calories**: 230
- **Fat**: 9 g
- **Carbs**: 15 g
- **Protein**: 22 g
- **Fiber**: 3 g

Bison and Pea Pilaf

Prep Time: 15 minutes

Cook Time: 30 minutes

Makes: 4 cups

Ingredients:

- 1 lb. of ground bison
- 1 cup of frozen or fresh peas
- 1 cup of uncooked brown rice
- 2 cups of dog-safe, low-salt beef broth
- 1 tbsp of vegetable oil

Instructions:

1. Heat the oil in a large skillet over medium heat and brown the bison. Stir continuously to break the meat down.

2. Add the rice, peas, and broth and bring it to a boil.

3. Reduce the heat to low, put a lid on, and simmer for about 25 to 30 minutes, until the peas have softened and the rice has absorbed the broth.

4. Let it cool, then serve or store in the fridge for two to three days.

Nutrition Per Serving (1 cup):

- **Calories**: 300
- **Fat**: 10 g
- **Carbs**: 35 g
- **Protein**: 18 g
- **Fiber**: 3 g

Beef and Sweet Potato Mash

25. Beef and sweet potato mash. Source:
https://www.flickr.com/photos/wolfworld/242815871

Prep Time: 15 minutes

Cook Time: 45 minutes

Makes: 4 servings

Ingredients:

- 1 lb. of lean ground beef
- 1 peeled, cubed large sweet potato
- 1 cup of chopped kale
- ½ cup of water
- 1 tsp of olive oil
- ½ tsp of turmeric

Instructions:

1. Heat the olive oil in a large pan over medium heat.
2. Brown the beef, stirring to break it down.
3. Add the water and potato, put a lid on and simmer until the potato is soft, about 20 minutes.
4. Stir in the turmeric and kale, put the lid back on, and cook for five minutes.
5. Turn off the heat and mash it with a fork until it reaches the right consistency for your dog.
6. Cool it then serve, or store for up to four days in the fridge or a month in the freezer.

Nutrition Per Serving (1/4 of the recipe):

- **Calories**: 220
- **Fat**: 8 g
- **Carbs**: 11 g
- **Protein**: 26 g

- **Fiber:** 2 g

Turkey and Pumpkin Pie

Prep Time: 15 minutes

Cook Time: 30 minutes

Makes: 6

Ingredients:

- ½ lb. of cooked, shredded turkey breast
- 1 cup of pumpkin puree (not pumpkin spice)
- ¼ cup finely chopped celery
- ¼ cup of diced pear
- ¼ cup of trimmed, chopped green beans
- 2 tbsp of almond flour

Instructions:

1. Preheat your oven to 375°F and lightly oil an oven-proof dish.
2. Combine all the ingredients in a bowl, combining gently.
3. Transfer it to the prepped dish, smooth it over, and cook for half an hour until golden brown and firm.
4. Let it cool, then serve your dog.
5. Store in the refrigerator for no more than four days or freeze it for up to a month.

Nutrition Per Serving (1/6th of the recipe):

- **Calories**: 190

- **Fat**: 7 g
- **Carbs**: 15 g
- **Protein**: 18 g
- **Fiber**: 3 g

Duck and Veggie Stir-Fry

Prep Time: 10 minutes

Cook Time: 20 minutes

Makes: 1

Ingredients:

- ½ lb. of cooked, shredded duck breast
- 1 cup of cooked kale
- ¼ cup of diced butternut squash
- ¼ cup of diced pears
- ¼ cup of diced cucumber
- 2 tbsp of almond flour

Instructions:

1. Steam the butternut squash until soft – you can do this in the microwave.

2. Lightly oil a skillet, heat it over medium heat, and sauté the squash, kale, pears, and cucumber until fork tender.

3. Add the duck and flour, stir it in, and heat it through.

4. Serve cooled or store in the fridge for no more than three days.

Nutrition Per Serving:

- **Calories**: 205
- **Fat**: 9 g
- **Carbs**: 16 g
- **Protein**: 19 g
- **Fiber**: 4 g

Turkey and Lentil Loaf

Prep Time: 15 minutes

Cook Time: 40 minutes

Makes: 1

Ingredients:

- ½ lb. of ground turkey
- 1 cup of lentils
- ¼ cup of diced carrots
- ¼ cup of finely chopped apple (cored and seeds removed)
- ¼ cup of peas
- 2 tbsp of almond flour

Instructions:

1. Preheat your oven to 375°F and grease an oven-proof dish.
2. Heat a skillet and brown the turkey, stirring frequently to break it down.

3. Meanwhile, cook the carrots and peas separately and cook the lentils per the package directions.

4. Mash the peas and combine all the ingredients in one bowl, then transfer it all the prepped dish.

5. Bake for half an hour, until firm and browned.

6. Cool, then slice and serve your dog.

7. Leftovers can be stored in the refrigerator for two to three days or freeze it for up to one month.

Nutrition Per Serving:

- **Calories**: 260
- **Fat**: 8 g
- **Carbs**: 24 g
- **Protein**: 24 g
- **Fiber**: 6 g

Duck and Green Bean Surprise

Prep Time: 15 minutes

Cook Time: 30 minutes

Makes: 4 cups

Ingredients:

- 1 lb. of ground duck
- 1 cup of trimmed, chopped green beans
- 1 cup of uncooked quinoa
- 2 cups of dog-safe, low-salt chicken broth
- 1 tbsp of olive oil

Instructions:

1. Heat the olive oil over medium heat in a large stock pot.

2. Cook the duck until browned, stirring frequently to break it down.

3. Add the quinoa, beans, and broth, stir, and bring to a boil.

4. Reduce the heat to low, put the lid on, and simmer for half an hour until the beans have softened and the quinoa is fully cooked.

5. Allow it to cool then serve your dog.

6. Refrigerate the leftovers for up to three days.

Nutrition Per Serving (1 cup):

- **Calories**: 320
- **Fat**: 12 g
- **Carbs**: 30 g
- **Protein**: 20 g
- **Fiber**: 3 g

Salmon and Buckwheat Noodles

Prep Time: 15 minutes

Cook Time: 25 minutes

Makes: 1

Ingredients:

- ½ lb. cooked, flaked skinless salmon fillet
- 1 cup of buckwheat noodles

- ¼ cup of chopped kale
- ¼ cup of diced bell peppers
- 2 tbsp of pumpkin seeds
- 1 tbsp of olive oil

Instructions:

1. Cook the noodles per the package instructions, then drain them.
2. Combine all the ingredients, except the pumpkin seeds, until thoroughly mixed.
3. Top with seeds and serve.
4. This can be stored in the fridge for no more than two days.

Nutrition Per Serving:

- **Calories**: 280
- **Fat**: 12 g
- **Carbs**: 18 g
- **Protein**: 22 g
- **Fiber**: 3 g

Chicken and Pumpkin

Prep Time: 10 minutes

Cook Time: 40 minutes

Makes: 6 cups

Ingredients:

- 1 lb. of skinless, boneless chicken breast

- 3 cups of water
- 1 cup of cubed pumpkin
- ½ cup of cooked rice
- ¼ cup of finely chopped carrots
- 1 tbsp of olive oil
- ½ tsp of ground ginger

Instructions:

1. Put the water and chicken in a large pot and let it come to a boil over medium heat.
2. Turn the heat down and simmer the chicken for about 20 minutes until cooked through.
3. Lift the chicken and set it aside to cool before shredding it.
4. Put the rice, pumpkin, and carrots in the water and bring it back to a boil.
5. Cook for about 20 minutes until the veggies are tender, then add the shredded chicken.
6. Add the ginger and olive oil, simmer for 10 minutes, then let it cool down to room temperature.
7. This can be stored in an airtight container for up to five days in the fridge or in the freezer for up to two months.

Nutrition Per Serving (1 cup):

- **Calories**: 55
- **Fat**: 2 g
- **Carbs**: 3 g
- **Protein**: 8 g

- **Fiber**: 0.5 g

Beef and Buckwheat

Prep Time: 15 minutes

Cook Time: 35 minutes

Makes: 4 servings

Ingredients:

- ½ lb. of lean ground beef
- 1 cup of cooked buckwheat
- ¼ cup of finely chopped broccoli
- ¼ cup of diced zucchini
- ¼ cup of blueberries
- 2 tbsp of low-fat cottage cheese

Instructions:

1. Preheat your oven to 375°F and place a sheet of baking powder on an oven-proof dish.

2. Heat a skillet and cook the beef, stirring frequently to break it down., then drain off the fat.

3. Mix all the ingredients in a bowl and place the mixture in the dish.

4. Bake for about 2 minutes or until slightly crispy around the edges.

5. Cool before serving.

6. This can be refrigerated for up to four days or frozen for two months.

Nutrition Per Serving (¼ of the recipe):

- **Calories**: 250
- **Fat**: 10 g
- **Carbs**: 20 g
- **Protein**: 20 g
- **Fiber**: 3 g

Lamb and Apple Delights

Prep Time: 15 minutes

Cook Time: 25 minutes

Makes: 24 treats

Ingredients:

- 1 cup of lean ground lamb
- 1 apple
- 1 cup of brown rice flour
- 1 egg

Instructions:

1. Heat your oven to 350°F and place baking paper on a cookie tray.
2. Heat a skillet and cook the lamb, stirring until it is broken down and browned.
3. Peel, core, and grate the apple.
4. Drain the fat from the lamb and put the meat in a bowl. Add the apple, egg, and flour, and stir to combine into a dough.

5. Flour a clean surface and roll the dough out about ¼-inch thick.

6. Cut it into 24 shapes using a cutter of your choice.

7. Place the treats on the prepped tray and bake for about 15 minutes until light brown.

8. Let them cool right down and store them in an airtight container for up to one week.

Nutrition Per Serving (1 treat):

- **Calories**: 65

- **Fat**: 3.5 g

- **Carbs**: 4 g

- **Protein**: 4 g

- **Fiber**: 1 g

Nutrition per treat: Calories: 65kcal; Fat: 3.5g; Carbs: 4g; Protein: 4g

---

Tuna and Spinach Croquettes

26. Tuna and spinach croquettes. Source:
https://www.flickr.com/photos/ysn/8379241141

Prep Time: 15 minutes

Cook Time: 0 minutes

Makes: 12 croquettes

Ingredients:

1. 1 cup of tuna canned in water
2. 1 cup of finely chopped spinach
3. ½ cup of oat flour
4. 1 egg
5. 1 tbsp of finely chopped fresh parsley

Instructions:

1. Drain the tuna and flake it.
2. Add it to a bowl with the spinach, flour, parsley, and egg. If you can't get oat flour, put rolled oats through a vegetable chopper or blender until they are finely ground.
3. Combine everything into a dough and make 12 croquettes from the mixture.
4. Line a baking sheet with baking paper and lay the croquettes on it.
5. Refrigerate for about an hour until firm.
6. These can be stored in an airtight container for up to five days in the fridge.

Nutrition Per Serving (1 croquette):

- **Calories**: 45
- **Fat**: 1.5 g
- **Carbs**: 3 g

- **Protein**: 5 g
- **Fiber**: 0.5 g

Cod and Lentil Stew

Prep Time: 10 minutes

Cook Time: 40 minutes

Makes: 1

Ingredients:

- ½ lb. of cooked, flaked cod
- 1 cup of lentils
- ¼ cup of diced sweet potato
- ¼ cup of chopped kale
- ¼ cup of water
- 2 tbsp of low-fat cottage cheese
- 1 tbsp of olive oil

Instructions:

1. Cook the lentils per the directions on the packet.
2. Cook the potato until soft.
3. Put all the ingredients, except the cottage cheese, in one bowl, stir to combine them, and bring to a simmer. Cook over low heat for about 40 minutes until it thickens.
4. Just before serving, add the cottage cheese and stir it in.

5. Serve warm or let it cool completely and store in the freezer or in the fridge for up to four days.

Nutrition Per Serving:

- **Calories**: 220
- **Fat**: 5 g
- **Carbs**: 23 g
- **Protein**: 21 g
- **Fiber: 6 g**

Chapter 7: Seasonal and Special Occasion Treats

Dogs deserve the odd treat on special occasions as much as humans do, but while you can make some amazing seasonal treats for your dog, don't forget to include them in their daily rations. Too many owners feed treats in addition to main meals and then wonder why their dog ends up obese.

27. Every good dog deserves a special treat! Source: https://unsplash.com/photos/brown-and-white-short-coated-dog-biting-brown-wooden-stick-5w30IN-0Lzs

Pumpkin Apple Dog Treats

Prep Time: 20 minutes

Cook Time: 30 minutes

Makes: 16 treats

Ingredients:

- 2 1/3 cups of all-purpose or wholewheat flour
- 1 cup of apple, diced finely
- ½ cup of pumpkin
- ½ cup of water
- 1 egg
- 1 tsp of baking powder

Instructions:

1. Heat your oven to 350°F and place baking paper on a cookie sheet.
2. Whisk the baking powder and flour to a fine powder.
3. Add the apple, pumpkin, water, and egg and stir to incorporate everything – the dry ingredients must be moist.
4. Flour a clean surface and roll the dough out.
5. Use a cookie cutter of your choice to cut 16 treats and place them on the cookie sheet.
6. Bake until crisp, about half an hour, then let them cool right down before feeding your dog.
7. These can be stored in an airtight container in your fridge for up to a week.

Nutrition Per Serving (1 treat):

- **Calories**: 76
- **Fat**: 1 g
- **Carbs**: 15 g
- **Protein**: 2 g
- **Fiber**: 1 g

Pumpkin, Cranberry, and Turkey Dog Treats

Prep Time: 10 minutes

Cook Time: 25 minutes

Makes: 52 treats

Ingredients:

- 2 ½ cups of oat flour
- 2 cups of unbalanced almond flour
- 2 ½ ounce jar of turkey baby food
- ¼ cup of dried cranberries
- ¼ cup of roasted pumpkin seeds
- ¼ cup of turkey bone broth
- 1/3 cup of pumpkin puree
- 1 tbsp of melted coconut oil

Instructions:

1. Preheat your oven to 350°F and put a silicon baking mat on a cookie sheet.

2. Sieve the oat and almond flour into a bowl and whisk them together.

3. Chop the pumpkin seeds and cranberries and stir them into the flour.

4. Combine the bone broth, coconut oil, baby food, and pumpkin in a bowl and slowly add them to the dry ingredients, slowly stirring them with a wooden spoon.

5. Form the mixture into a dough using your hands and knead it for one or two minutes.

6. Lightly flour a sheet of wax paper and turn the dough out onto it.

7. Flatten it and roll it out ¼-inch thick.

8. Use a cookie cutter of your choice to cut the dough into 52 treats and place them onto the cookie sheet.

9. Bake for 25 minutes, then let them cool down completely.

10. Store in the fridge for up to a week in an airtight container.

Nutrition Per Serving (1 cookie):

- **Calories**: 57
- **Fat**: 2.9 g
- **Carbs**: 5.6 g
- **Protein**: 3.5 g
- **Fiber**: 1.1 g

Dog Breath Mints

Prep Time: 20 minutes

Cook Time: 40 minutes

Makes: 40 mints

Ingredients:

- 2 ½ cups of old-fashioned oats
- ½ cup of finely chopped parsley
- ½ cup of finely chopped fresh mint
- 1 large egg OR ¼ cup of unsweetened applesauce for dogs allergic to eggs
- ¼ cup + 1 tbsp of water
- 3 tbsp of melted coconut oil

Instructions:

1. Heat your oven to 325°F and line a cookie sheet with baking paper.

2. Pulse the oats in a blender until they resemble flour.

3. Whisk the mint, parsley, egg, oil, and ¼ cup of water in a bowl and stir in the oat flour.

4. If needed, add the remaining tbsp of water to help form the mixture into a dough.

5. Knead it a couple of times. Flour a clean surface, turn the dough out, and roll it 1/8-inch thick.

6. Cut the dough into 40 evenly sized pieces, about an inch square, and put them on the cookie sheet.

7. Bake until crispy and golden, about 35 to 40 minutes,

8. Cool them completely, then store them in a sealed container.

Nutrition Per Serving (1 mint):

- **Calories**: 30
- **Fat**: 1 g
- **Carbs**: 4 g
- **Protein**: 1 g
- **Fiber**: 1 g

Dog-Friendly Frosted Birthday Cake

28. Dog birthday cake! Source: https://unsplash.com/photos/brown-long-coated-dog-wearing-pink-and-white-polka-dot-shirt-h2VU6loJrNk

Prep Time: 15 minutes

Cook Time: 25 minutes

Makes: 20 to 30 Slices

Ingredients:

For the Cake:

- 2 eggs

- 2 ½ cups of shredded carrot

- 2 cups of whole wheat flour

- ½ cup of xylitol-free peanut butter

- ¼ cup of vegetable or canola oil

- 2/3 cup of milk OR water

- 1/3 cup of organic honey, maple syrup, or unsweetened applesauce

- 2 ½ tsp of baking soda

For the Frosting:

- 1.2 to 1.4 lb. of peeled, cubed potatoes

- ¾ - 1 cup of plain Greek yogurt OR water

Instructions:

1. Heat your oven to 350°F and prepare two 8-inch cake pans by greasing them and lining the bottom with baking paper.

2. Whisk the peanut butter, eggs, honey, milk, and oil together, then add the carrot and stir it in.

3. Stir in the baking soda and flour until the mixture is just combined – don't overmix, or the cake will be hard.

4. Transfer the batter to the pans, smooth it out, and bake for 25 minutes. A toothpick should come out clean when inserted in the center. If not, continue baking for a little longer.

5. Turn the cakes out onto a wire rack to cool.

6. Make the frosting. Cook the potato until it is falling apart.

7. Transfer it to a bowl, add the yogurt, and whip until smooth and fluffy – medium speed on an electric mixer for about 1 ½ minutes. Don't expect it to be completely smooth; just get it as close as possible.

8. If the frosting is a bit thick, add a little warm water to make it soft and spreadable.

9. Spread a quarter of the frosting over one cake and place the other on top. Use the rest of the frosting to coat the sides and top, keeping some back if you want to add some piped decorations.

10. Slice and store in an airtight container.

Note:

This must not be used as a meal replacement and must be included as part of their daily nutrition requirements, not given as an extra.

Nutrition Per Serving (1 slice):

- **Calories**: 157
- **Fat**: 6 g
- **Carbs**: 20 g
- **Protein**: 4 g
- **Fiber**: 1 g

Halloween Dog Treats

Prep Time: 15 minutes

Cook Time: 25 minutes

Makes: 24 - 36

Ingredients:

For the Treat:

- 5 cups of oat flour
- 2 eggs
- 1 cup of pumpkin puree
- ½ cup of unsweetened, xylitol-free peanut butter

For the Icing:

- Plant-based, dog-safe food coloring
- 2 tsp of activated charcoal powder – for black icing if required
- 1 tsp of organic honey
- 2 to 3 tbsp of arrowroot powder cornstarch or tapioca starch

Instructions:

1. Heat your oven to 350°F and line a large cookie sheet with baking paper or a silicon mat.

2. Put the flour, eggs, pumpkin, and peanut butter in a bowl and combine into a dough.

3. Turn the dough out onto a sheet of baking paper, place another sheet on top, and roll it out to ½-inch thick.

4. Use cookie cutters of your choice to cut the treats out and place them on the cookie sheet.

5. Gather the dough scraps, roll them again, and cut more shapes – continue until the dough is all gone.

6. Bake the treats for about 20 to 25 minutes until golden brown.

7. Set them aside to cool while you make the icing.

8. Make the colors you want following the instructions on the food coloring. Mix the charcoal powder with 1 tbsp of hot water if you want black icing.

9. Mix the honey with two tsp of food coloring and 2 tbsp of your thickener until smooth and thoroughly combined. Add more thickener or water if needed and drizzle it over the treats.

10. Let the coloring set before storing the treats in an airtight container in the fridge.

Nutrition Per Serving (1 treat):

- **Calories**: 97
- **Fat**: 1 g
- **Carbs**: 13 g
- **Protein**: 4 g
- **Fiber**: 1 g

Christmas Dog Treats

Prep Time: 25 minutes

Cook Time: 20 minutes

Makes: 12

Ingredients:

For the Treats:

- 2 cups of uncooked oatmeal

- 1 cup of whole wheat flour

- ¼ cup of melted coconut oil

- ½ cup of water

- 1 egg

- 1 tsp of ground ginger

- 1 tsp of ground cinnamon

For the Icing:

- ½ cup of tapioca starch

- ½ cup of plain Greek yogurt

Instructions:

1. Heat your oven to 350°F and place a silicon baking mat or baking powder on a cookie sheet.

2. Pulse the oatmeal to a fine flour consistency in a blender.

3. Combine the oat flour, wheat flour, coconut oil, egg, spice, and water in a stand mixer or use an electric mixer. You'll need to finish it with your hands to ensure everything is well combined.

4. Turn the dough out onto a lightly floured surface and roll it out to 1-4 to ½-inch thick.

5. Use a holiday cookie cutter to cut out shapes and place them on the prepped sheet. Continue until all the dough is used.

6. Bake for 20 to 25 minutes, then turn them onto a wire rack to cool.

7. Combine the yogurt and starch to make the icing. Transfer it to a piping bag and decorate the treats. Store in an airtight container.

NOTES

Do not substitute the spices for nutmeg, as this is a toxic substance for dogs.

If you don't have tapioca starch, you can use rice flour, potato flour, or cornstarch.

If you want to color the icing, use the following:

- **Red:** beetroot powder, natural cherry juice, or strawberries
- **Green:** spirulina powder, parsley, or spinach

Alternatively, use dog-safe, natural food coloring.

Nutrition Per Serving (1 treat):

- **Calories**: 130
- **Fat**: 6 g
- **Carbs**: 17 g
- **Protein**: 4 g
- **Fiber**: 2 g

Gingerbread Dog Treats

Prep Time: 20 minutes

Cook Time: 25 minutes

Makes: 36

Ingredients:

- 2 cups of raw, old-fashioned rolled oats
- 1 cup of brown rice flour
- ¼ cup of melted coconut oil
- ½ cup of water
- 1 egg
- 1 tsp of ground ginger
- 1 tsp of ground cinnamon

Instructions:

1. Heat your oven to 350°F and prepare a cookie sheet with baking paper or a silicon mat.

2. Put the oats in a food processor or blender and pulse to a fine flour-like consistency.

3. Put the flour in a bowl and add the rice flour and spices. Whisk to combine.

4. Add the coconut oil, egg, and water and whisk to combine.

5. Lightly flour a surface and turn the dough out onto it.

6. Roll it out to ¼ to ½-inch thick and use a cookie cutter to cut out treats. Use all the dough, place the treats on the prepped sheet, and bake for 20 to 25 minutes. Turn the treats out onto a wire rack and let them cool before storing them in an airtight container.

Nutrition Per Serving (1 treat):

- **Calories**: 48
- **Fat**: 2 g

- **Carbs**: 7 g
- **Protein**: 1 g
- **Fiber**: 1 g

Thanksgiving Dog Treats

Prep Time: 20 minutes

Cook Time: 20 minutes

Makes: 20

Ingredients:

- 1 cup of cooked, shredded plain turkey
- ¾ cup of brown rice flour
- ½ cup of cooked, chopped green beans
- ½ cup of cooked, mashed sweet potato
- 1 egg

Instructions:

1. Heat your oven to 350°F and prepare a cookie sheet with baking paper.
2. Put the turkey, beans, egg, and potato in a blender and pulse until combined.
3. Transfer it to a bowl and fold the green beans in.
4. Stir in the flour gradually until you have a pliable dough.
5. Flour a clean surface and roll the dough out to ¼ to ½-inch thick.

6. Cut out your desired shapes, using all the dough, and put the treats on the cookie sheet.

7. Bake for 20 to 25 minutes, then cool the teats on a wire rack before storing them in an airtight container or bag.

NOTE

The sweet potato must be plain – do not use candied or casserole sweet potatoes as these contain ingredients your dog should not eat.

Nutrition Per Serving (1 treat):

- **Calories**: 36
- **Fat**: 1 g
- **Carbs**: 5 g
- **Protein**: 2 g
- **Fiber**: 0.4 g

Easter Dog Treats

Prep Time: 5 minutes

Cook Time: 20 minutes

Makes: 120 treats

Ingredients:

For Carob Treats:

- 1 cup of unsweetened carob chips
- ½ cup of coconut oil

For Peanut Butter Carob Treats:

- 1 cup of xylitol-free, creamy peanut butter
- 1 cup of unsweetened carob chips

Instructions:

You can make these in two ways.

Carob Treats:

1. Using a double boiler: melt the oil in the top of a double boiler and stir in half the carob chips. Continue stirring and heating until they are melted, then add the rest and heat until the mixture is smooth.

2. Using a microwave: melt the coconut oil in the microwave for 15 seconds, then add half the carob and stir. Continue heating for 30 seconds, stir, and repeat until melted. Add the rest of the chips and repeat until you have a smooth combined mixture.

Carob Peanut Butter Treats:

1. Using a double boiler: heat the peanut butter in the top of a double boiler, stirring until melted, then gradually add the carob chips. Stir consistently until melted and combined.

2. Using a microwave: melt the peanut butter for 15 to 20 seconds, then stir in half the carob chips. Heat for 30 seconds, stir, and repeat until fully melted. Stir in the rest of the carob chips and continue heating and stirring until melted. If it is too thick, add a little melted coconut oil.

3. Place a silicon mold tray onto a baking sheet and pour the mixture in carefully,

4. Refrigerate until hard, about half an hour.

5. Turn the hardened treats out of the molds and store them in the fridge in an airtight container.

Nutrition Per Serving (1 treat):

- **Calories**: 37
- **Fat**: 3 g
- **Carbs**: 2 g
- **Protein**: 1 g
- **Fiber**: 0.2 g

Valentine Dog Treats

Prep Time: 20 minutes

Cook Time: 20 minutes

Makes: 15

Ingredients:

For the Treats:

- 3 cups of oat flour
- ½ cup of unsweetened applesauce
- ¼ cup of xylitol-free peanut butter
- 1 egg
- 1 tbsp of melted coconut oil

For the Icing:

- 2 tbsp of natural coloring or beet powder – see notes
- 2 tsp of water
- 1 tsp of organic honey

- 2 tbsp of cornstarch, tapioca starch, or arrowroot powder + extra if required

Instructions:

1. Heat your oven to 350°F and prepare a cookie sheet with a silicon mat or baking paper.

2. Combine the applesauce, peanut butter, egg, and coconut oil using a hand whisk or electric mixer.

3. Gradually add in the oat flour, whisking to combine.

4. Turn the dough out onto a floured surface and roll it out to ½-inch thick.

5. Cut as many heart-shaped cookies as possible, then gather the dough, roll it out again, and cut more. Repeat until all the dough is used.

6. Lay the cookies on the prepped sheet and bake for 12 to 15 minutes.

7. Turn them out onto a wire rack and let them cool while you make the icing.

8. Mix the water and beet powder and put two teaspoons in a bowl. Add the honey and two teaspoons of thickener and mix thoroughly. Add more thickener if needed to get a spreadable icing.

9. Spread the icing over the cooled cookies, let it harden, and then store them in an airtight container in the fridge.

NOTE

Natural food coloring can be made by simmering ¼ cup of strawberries, beets, or raspberries until all the juices are released. Use more for a darker coloring or less for a lighter coloring. Strain the liquid and add water to make two teaspoons of coloring.

Nutrition Per Serving (1 treat):

- **Calories**: 135
- **Fat**: 1 g
- **Carbs**: 19 g
- **Protein**: 5 g
- **Fiber**: 2 g

Sweet Potato Pie

Prep Time: 20 minutes

Cook Time: 18 minutes

Makes: 12

Ingredients:

For the Crust:

- ¾ cup of oat flour
- ½ cup of unsweetened applesauce
- 1 egg

For the Filling:

- ¾ cup of plain, cooked, and mashed sweet potato
- 1 egg
- 1 tsp of ground cinnamon

For the Topping:

- ¼ cup of plain Greek yogurt

Instructions:

1. Heat your oven to 350°F and grease the cups of a 12-cup mini muffin pan or use silicon muffin liners.

2. Mix the egg, applesauce, and flour in a bowl, and put about one tablespoon of the mixture into each muffin cup. Press it down in the center and up around the sides of each cup.

3. Bake them for eight minutes while you make the filling.

4. Combine the egg, cinnamon, and applesauce in a small bowl. When the crusts are cooked, spoon a teaspoon or so into each cup and bake for 10 minutes.

5. Let the pies cool to room temperature before spooning a little Greek yogurt on top of each one just before serving.

6. These can be stored in the fridge for up to four days in an airtight container. Alternatively, store them in the freezer for up to three months.

Nutrition Per Serving (1 pie):

- **Calories**: 55
- **Fat**: 1 g
- **Carbs**: 8 g
- **Protein**: 3 g
- **Fiber**: 1 g

Chapter 8: DIY Supplements and Additions

When a dog is off-color, suffering with their joints, or any number of other complaints, you should seek advice from your vet. However, sometimes, you can use natural supplements instead of tablets and injections from your vet. This chapter offers you some great ideas and recipes for natural, completely safe supplements you can add to your dog's food.

29. DIY supplements. Source: https://www.pexels.com/photo/dog-treat-in-the-shape-of-bones-13382042/

Golden Turmeric Paste

Golden paste is an excellent natural anti-inflammatory that can help your dog maintain healthy joints.

Prep Time: 5 minutes

Cook Time: 24 minutes

Makes: 24 servings

Ingredients:

- 1 cup of water
- ¼ cup of ground turmeric powder
- ¼ cup of coconut oil
- 1 ½ tsp of freshly ground black pepper

Instructions:

1. Put the turmeric and water in a saucepan, stir, and heat over medium-high heat. When it comes to a boil, turn the heat down and simmer it for about 10 minutes. Stir occasionally to help it form into a paste.

2. Take the pan off the heat and set it aside for 5 to 10 minutes to cool.

3. Stir the pepper and coconut oil in until thoroughly combined and set it aside until it reaches room temperature.

4. Put the paste in an airtight container and refrigerate for up to two weeks or freeze it for up to four months.

NOTES

Do not use pre-ground pepper as it has been exposed to air and light, which degrades the piperine in it – the important ingredient.

Be aware that turmeric stains anything it touches, so clean up immediately after using it and try to dedicate a set of utensils and cloths purely for use with turmeric.

Recipe Variations

- Use bone broth instead of water.
- When you add the pepper, stir in up to one tablespoon of ground ginger or Ceylon cinnamon. Never use Cassia cinnamon, as it isn't safe.

How to Use:

Mix it with a little water before adding it to your dog's food.

- **Small Dogs:** start with ¼ tsp per day
- **Medium Dogs:** start with ½ tsp per day
- **Large Dogs:** start with ¾ tsp per day
- **Giant Dogs:** start with 1 tsp per day

Gradually increase it if your dog can tolerate it. You can safely give your dog 1/8 to ¼-tsp per 10 lb. of weight per day. For example, a 40lb dog can have ½ to 1 tsp but increase it gradually.

Bone Broth for Dogs

Bone broth is great for overall health, including a shiny coat, healthy skin, digestive system, joints, and more. It also adds extra flavor to your dog's food and can be used in recipes instead of other liquids, like water.

Prep Time: 5 minutes

Cook Time: 24 hours

Makes: 16 servings

Ingredients:

- 2 lb. of bones – chicken back bones, thighs, feet, wings, turkey necks, turkey carcass, etc.

- 4 large carrots chopped into chunks

- 4 celery stalks cut into chunks

- ¼ cup of apple cider vinegar

- water

Instructions:

1. Put all the bones in a large stock pot, add the veggies, and cover them with water to an inch above them. Add the vinegar and bring it to a boil.

2. Turn the heat down to low, cover the pot, and simmer it for 24 hours. During the first hour, skim off the foam from the top. Check on it now and then and add more water if it drops below the top of the ingredients.

3. After 24 hours, strain the broth into a large mixing bowl and discard the solids.

4. Fill up your sink with cold water and ice and stand the mixing bowl in it for about 15 minutes, stirring often. Use a meat thermometer to test the broth temperature, and when it reaches 50°F, lift the bowl from the ice.

5. Transfer the broth to an airtight container and store it in the fridge overnight.

6. Before using it, remove the hard fat cap from the top, leaving you with a thick jelly-like liquid.

7. Heat it in a microwave to warm it up before use.

Brewer's Yeast Herb Blend

Homemade brewer's yeast blend contains nutrients and protects your dog from fleas.

Prep Time: 5 minutes

Cook Time: 5 minutes

Makes: 64 servings

Ingredients:

- 1 cup of brewer's yeast
- ¼ cup of dried parsley
- 1 tsp of dried thyme
- 1 tsp of dried rosemary
- 1 tsp of dried sage
- 1 tsp of dried dill weed

Instructions:

1. Put the thyme and rosemary in a coffee or spice grinder and pulse it to a powder. You can do this to all the herbs if you want.

2. Mix everything and store it in an airtight container.

3. Mix the blend into your dog's food at ½ tsp per 10 lb. of weight per day.

Coconut Treats

These are great for keeping your dog's skin healthy and making the coat shiny.

Prep Time: 10 minutes

Freeze Time: 2 hours

You will need silicon molds or ice cube trays with small molds.

Ingredients:

- ¼ cup of organic coconut oil – see note
- ½ cup of powdered brewer's yeast

Instructions:

1. Place the silicon molds or ice cube trays on a baking tray.
2. Melt the coconut oil in the microwave – use a container with a pour spout, like a microwave-safe jug.
3. Melt the oil for 30 seconds, then stir it and repeat until it is smooth and melted.
4. Add the yeast and stir to incorporate it, making sure there are no lumps.
5. Pour the mixture into the molds and place in the freezer or fridge to harden. The yeast will settle at the bottom with the oil at the top.
6. Once hard, transfer them to a sealable jar and store them in the freezer or fridge for up to six months.

NOTES

Do not use unrefined coconut oil, as it is less nutritious than organic, raw oil.

Do not heat the oil too much, as heat destroys the nutrients.

Be aware that coconut oil can lead to weight gain if too much is fed. It can also cause pancreatitis or diarrhea, so do not overfeed. Feed at a rate of 1 tsp of oil and ½ tsp of yeast per 10 lb. of weight.

Start with feeding these every other day but if your dog develops diarrhea, cease feeding them.

Homemade Oil Supplement

Great for joints and healthy coat and skin.

Prep Time: 10 minutes

Cook Time: 0 minutes

Makes: 1 ¾ cups

Ingredients:

- ½ cup of canola oil
- ½ cup of flaxseed oil
- ½ cup of olive oil
- ¼ cup of castor oil

Instructions:

1. Mix everything in one airtight container and shake it well.

---

2. Keep it in the refrigerator until needed and shake before use.

3. Feed ½ tsp per 20 lb. of weight per day with meals.

Eggshell Calcium Powder

30. Eggshell Calcium powder. Source:
https://www.pexels.com/photo/white-eggs-flour-on-top-of-a-table-8477774/

Instructions:

1. As you use eggs, wash the shells and put them in a bowl. If you don't wash them, the inner membrane can smell and become moldy.

2. When ready to use them, bake the eggshells at 300°F for five to seven minutes, or add them to a pot of boiling water for five minutes.

3. Spread them out to dry thoroughly.

4. Grind them into a powder using a coffee or spice grinder, blender, food processor, or pestle and mortar.

Sprinkle a little on your dog's food daily.

Pureed Fruits and Veggies

Fresh pureed fruits and veggies provide additional flavor, are great for enticing picky pups, and add extra nutrients to your pup's diet.

However, you shouldn't use too much, as dogs traditionally wouldn't eat a whole lot of plant matter in their diets. Replace no more than five to ten of their daily food with pureed produce.

Some of the best are boiled sweet potatoes, raw bell peppers, celery, carrots, apples (no core or seeds), and strawberries, as they offer minerals, vitamins, and antioxidants.

If your dog has been diagnosed with cancer, only puree non-starchy, low-carb produce, such as raspberries, blackberries, cauliflower, Brussels sprouts, Shiitake mushrooms, and broccoli.

Chapter 9: Kong Stuffing Ideas

Kongs are a great invention, as they can help keep your bored pup occupied and entertained for hours on end, depending on what you stuff with them. They are also excellent stress-reducers, and they help your dog maintain a healthy set of teeth. You can stuff them with many different things, and this chapter provides some amazing ideas.

31. Kongs can keep your pup occupied and if you make them at home they're super healthy too. Source: https://www.pexels.com/photo/shallow-focus-photo-of-long-coated-white-and-gray-puppy-2174209/

Peanut Butter and Banana Kong

Ingredients:

- 1 banana

- 1 cup of plain, unsweetened Greek yogurt

- 2 tbsp of xylitol-free peanut butter

Instructions:

1. Slice the banana or chop it into small bits. Overripe bananas can be mashed.

2. Combine it with the yogurt.

3. Heat the peanut butter in the microwave until a pourable consistency is reached, then mix it into the yogurt and banana.

4. Seal the hole at the narrow point of the kong with a small amount of cold peanut butter.

5. Transfer the mixture into the kong, packing it as tight as you can, then wrap it in sandwich bags or plastic wrap and freeze overnight – make sure the large hole is facing upward.

6. Give it to your dog frozen – it will keep them entertained for hours.

Kong Delights

Ingredients:

Yogurt and Blueberry:

- 1 cup of low-fat, plain, unsweetened yogurt

- Handful of frozen or fresh blueberries

Cookie Crunch:

- 1 cup of low-fat plain cottage cheese

- 1 cup of plain, low-fat, unsweetened yogurt

- A handful of dog cookies

Coconut and Banana:

- 1 cup of mashed banana

- 1 cup of low-fat, plain, unsweetened yogurt

- 2 tbsp of unrefined coconut oil

Instructions:

1. Mix the ingredients of your chosen recipe.

2. Seal the small hole in the kong with peanut butter, then stuff the kong with the ingredients.

3. Wrap it in plastic and freeze it upright overnight.

Chicken and Sweet Potato Kong Filler

Ingredients:

- ½ cup of white rice, cooked

- 1 small sweet potato

- 2 tbsp of dog-safe chicken stock or warmed bone broth

- ¼ tsp of organic honey

- ¼ tsp of peanut butter

- 1 dog biscuit or treat

Instructions:

1. Peel the potato and cut it into cubes of about an inch.

2. Put the cubes in a pot, add enough water to cover them by an inch, and bring them to a boil. Cook until fork-tender, then drain and put them in a bowl.

3. Stir the rice, honey, and stock into the potatoes, mashing them all together until smooth.

4. Use peanut butter to plug the small hole in the kong and spoon the rest of the mixture into the kong. Pack it in tight and pop the treat or biscuit into the mixture.

5. Give to your dog as it or freeze it first, wrapped in plastic or stood, small-end down, in a freezer-safe mug.

Coconut Banana-Strawberry Frosty Kong

Ingredients:

- 1 tsp of unrefined coconut oil

- 1 sliced banana

- ½ cup of sliced strawberries

- 1 cup of unsweetened plain yogurt

Instructions:

1. Add everything to a blender and mix to a smooth puree.

2. Block the small end of the kong with a little peanut butter and pour the mixture in.

3. Freeze upright for at least two hours before giving it to your dog.

Chicken Casserole Kong

Ingredients:

- 1 sweet potato
- 2 large carrots
- ¼ cup of green beans
- Chicken stock
- Plain unsweetened yogurt

Instructions:

1. Wash the vegetables and dice them into small pieces.
2. Cook them until soft, then drain and put them in a bowl.
3. Add a few spoons of yogurt and stir a little chicken stock in, creating a saucy mix.
4. Block the small hole in the kong and pour the mixture in.
5. Freeze upright overnight.

Apple Pie Stuffing

Ingredients:

- 2 ¾ cups of wheat pastry flour
- 4 cups of cored, peeled, and sliced apples
- 1 cup of unsweetened coconut milk
- ½ cup of melted coconut oil
- 1/3 cup of water

- 1 tbsp of cornstarch

- 2 tsp of ground cinnamon

Instructions:

1. Heat the oven to 350°F and grease the cups on a 6-cup muffin tin.

2. Make the crust by combining the flour with the milk and coconut oil.

3. Flour a surface and roll out the dough to ¼-inch thick. Cut and press it into the muffin cups, covering the base and sides.

4. Put the apples in a saucepan with two tablespoons of water and cook over low heat.

5. Mix the cinnamon, remaining water, and cornstarch in a bowl and pour it into the pan with the softened apples. Stir and let it cook for about 10 minutes.

6. Let it cool, scoop it into the cups, and make lattice tops for each one if you have any leftover dough.

7. Bake for 25 to 30 minutes, then let them cool right down.

8. Stuff the kong with pie and give it to your pup.

Banana Cheesecake Kong

Ingredients:

- ½ to 1 cup of dog treats

- 1 tbsp of low-fat, plain cream cheese

- 1 tbsp of low-fat, plain, unsweetened yogurt

- 2 tsp of salmon oil
- ½ a sliced banana

Instructions:

1. Put the dog treats in a blender or grinder and process to a fine powder.

2. Transfer it to a bowl and stir in the salmon oil.

3. Block the small end of the kong with a little peanut butter and press it into the bottom to form the crust.

4. Blend the banana, yogurt, and cream cheese and press it into the kong on top of the crust.

5. Add banana slices to garnish and freeze upright for a couple of hours.

Candy Corn

Ingredients:

- 1 cup of pumpkin puree
- 1 cup of plain, unsweetened yogurt
- 1 tbsp of organic maple syrup
- 1 tsp of ground cinnamon
- 1 cup of mashed banana

Instructions:

1. Spoon the mashed banana over the base of a shallow silicon pan and freeze it for 20 minutes.

2. Combine the pumpkin and cinnamon and spread it on top of the banana. Freeze for 20 minutes.

3. Combine the syrup and yogurt and spread it over the pumpkin.

4. Freeze for up to two hours, then cut it into small pieces.

5. Stuff the kong with the candy corn pieces and give it to your dog.

Apple Cheddar Pupcakes

Ingredients:

- ½ cup of shredded cheddar
- ½ cup of unsweetened applesauce
- ¼ cup of diced apple – no seeds
- ½ cup of raw rolled oats
- 2 tbsp of organic honey

Instructions:

1. Combine everything in a bowl until fully mixed.

2. Block the small end of the kong with peanut butter and fill it with the apple mixture.

3. Freeze upright for a couple of hours before giving it to your pup.

Birthday Carrot Cake

Ingredients:

- ½ a cup of oatmeal
- ½ a cup of grated carrot
- ½ a cup of unsweetened applesauce

- 1 tbsp of low-fat cream cheese
- 1 tsp of ground cinnamon

Instructions:

1. Combine all the ingredients in a bowl.
2. Use peanut butter to block the small hole and fill the kong with the mixture.
3. Freeze for a couple of hours or give it to your pup as is.

Summer Picnic

Ingredients:

- 1 cup of cooked ground turkey
- ½ cup of grated carrot
- ½ cup of low-fat cream cheese

Instructions:

1. Mix all the ingredients thoroughly and stuff it into the kong.
2. Freeze first or feed it to your pup straight away.

Kong-U-Copia

Ingredients:

- ½ a diced apple
- 2 to 3 baby carrots
- ½ cup of fresh, frozen, or canned corn
- 3 to 4 tbsp of pumpkin puree

Instructions:

1. Combine all the ingredients in a bowl.

2. Spoon it into the kong and feed it to your pup or freeze it first.

Mother's Day Breakfast

Ingredients:

- ½ cup of plain scrambled eggs

- ½ cup of shredded potato

- ½ cup of crumbled turkey sausage

Instructions:

1. Combine all the ingredients.

2. Stuff the mixture into your kong and freeze or feed straight away.

Pumpkin Pie

Ingredients:

- 3/8 cup of shredded carrot

- 1/8 cup of cubed apple

- ¼ cup of pureed pumpkin

Instructions:

1. Fill half the kong width with apple cubes.

2. Mix the rest of the ingredients and stuff them into the kong.

3. Feed as is or freeze first.

Chapter 10: Frequently Asked Questions

By now, you should have realized that feeding your dog a homemade fresh diet is the best thing you could do for your best friend. Not only will you provide them with tasty food every day, but you will also be doing them the world of good in terms of health and well-being.

However, you may still have questions or want some clarification on some points, and these frequently asked questions and answers will help you get the information you want.

Let's dive in and get your questions answered:

1. How Much Should A Dog Be Fed?

Typically, you should feed your dog 2 to 3% of their ideal weight. For example, if your dog is underweight, work out (or ask your vet) how much they should weigh, and then use that figure to work out the percentages—the same works for overweight dogs.

Here's a chart to help you work it out:

One pound is equal to two cups.

Ideal Weight	Feeding Guidelines
100 lb.	2 to 3 lb. per day divided into two meals
75 lb.	1 ½ to 2 ¾ lb. per day divided into two meals
50 lb.	1 to 1 1/82 lb. per day divided into two meals
25 lb.	8 to 12 ounces per day divided into two meals

2. Can Protein Sources be Substituted for Others?

Absolutely. So long as the substitution is dog-friendly and meaty, you can use any protein you want. People commonly do this to use cheaper meat than the recipe suggests or because their dog is allergic to a certain protein.

Commonly, dog food recipes contain chicken, beef, and turkey, but some dogs are allergic to one or more of these. Instead, you could use venison, rabbit, lamb, goat, and bison.

3. Apart from Proteins, Can Other Ingredients Be substituted?

Yes, they can, but as there are more alternatives in carbs and fresh produce, you will need to consider what you use carefully. You also need to ensure that the nutritional value of your dog's food is correct.

Carbohydrates:

Commercial foods are mostly carbohydrates, but on the whole, your dog doesn't really need that much. However, carbs are also rich in nutrients and fiber and won't harm your dog. The small intestine breaks carbs into small glucose molecules, a good energy source most of the dog's cells will use. The brain and nervous system also require glucose.

So long as the carbs you include are dog-friendly, they will not harm your pet. Common sources are cereal grains, including:

- Barley
- Brown rice
- Corn
- Oats
- Sweet potato
- White potato
- Whole wheat

Fruits/Veggies:

Your dog's meals should also contain a certain amount of fruits and vegetables. These are chock full of the minerals and vitamins your dog needs, but not all are safe for your dog. When you want to substitute ingredients, you need to make sure you only use dog-safe ingredients, including:

- Apples
- Blueberries
- Bananas
- Cantaloupe melon
- Mango
- Broccoli
- Bell pepper

- Carrots

- Peas

- Green beans

- Zucchini

Fat:

Most people consider fat bad, but some fats are healthy, and dogs need a certain amount of them in their diet. On average, the diet should be 10 to 15% healthy fat. Too little can leave your dog with itchy skin and a dry coat, and too much will lead to obesity. When you want to substitute fat sources, these are the healthiest and safest ones to use:

- Canola oil

- Flaxseed oil

- Sunflower oil

- Coconut oil

- Poultry fat

- Soybean oil

- Fish oils

No matter what subs you must make or why, ensure your dog's diet is still nutritionally correct.

4. Is Brown Rice Healthier Than White for Dogs?

There really isn't a right way to answer that except to say that both are fine, and each has its own benefits. Dogs can chew and digest white rice easier, and it is generally cheaper than brown rice, but brown rice has more starch and protein and is considered nutritionally better because it is a whole, unprocessed grain. It also has a lot more fiber, which can lead to an upset stomach if your dog consumes too much.

Bottom line – feed your dog whichever one fits the situation. White rice is excellent when your dog has an upset stomach, while brown rice is good when your dog is constipated or needs to gain a little weight. Just ensure that whatever rice you choose is properly cooked.

5. How Can I Make My Dog's Meals Balanced in Nutrition with Supplements?

To answer that, you first need to understand the nutritional balance in your dog's diet:

- **Protein:** Typically found in eggs, dairy, seafood, and meat. Your dog's diet should contain a minimum of 25 to 35% of good-quality protein. You can reduce the carb content and increase in protein, but use lean sources to avoid increasing the fat content. Organ meats are also a good choice.

- **Carbs:** Cereal grains, beans, vegetables, and fruits. 30 to 50% of your dog's diet can be carbs, but it doesn't need to be. Just make sure they are nutritional sources.

- **Fats:** Fatty fish, fatty meats, and oils. Fat should be no more than 10 to 20% of the diet and should be from healthy sources. They provide energy and you should include fish to get omega-3s.

- **Vitamins and Minerals:** Vegetables, fruits, meat, and grains – particularly organ meat. Dogs require some minerals and vitamins more than they do others, particularly phosphorus and calcium at certain life stages and less in other stages. Do your research!

Supplements are commonly used in homemade diets, commonly calcium, as dogs need it in high amounts. They won't get much unless your dog eats kibble or raw bones. Adding ground-up eggshells can help.

Your dog also needs sodium, phosphorus, potassium, magncsium, chloride, sulfur, Vitamin A, and vitamin E. If those are not provided in his daily meals, you will need to add supplements. Do seek advice from your vet first.

6. Can Supplements Take the Place of Protein or Fruits and Veggies?

No. If you do, you won't be doing your dog any favors. If your dog is allergic to a certain food, there are plenty of other safe alternatives you can use to provide your dog with what he needs. In most cases, these substitutes are much cheaper than supplements and are far healthier, providing your dog with natural sources of vitamins and minerals. You can use small amounts of protein supplements but never whey protein, as it is made from milk and wheat sources and is not ideal for their digestive system.

In terms of fruit and veggies, supplements can be used instead but it still isn't advisable. There is little evidence to show supplements are healthier and dogs can't always absorb supplements. If you are concerned about mineral and vitamin intake, you can always add pureed fruits and veggies to your dog's diet or give them raw ones as a treat.

7. How Should a Dog Be Transitioned to a Homemade Diet?

The obvious answer is slowly. A sudden and complete change to your dog's diet won't do him any favors. Instead, it should be done over time. When your dog is fed on a commercial diet, you should be careful – suddenly switching to a homemade diet can affect his health, especially if you don't take care of how it's done. While some dogs seem to be able to eat anything with no consequences, others have trouble adapting to new diets. The best option is to take it slow and steady to ensure your dog can easily adapt. Here's the best way to do it:

- **Day One:** 90% old diet and 10% new food
- **Day Two:** 80% old diet and 20% new food
- **Day Three:** 70% old diet and 30% new food
- **Day Four:** 60% old diet and 40% new food
- **Day Five:** 40% old diet and 60% new food
- **Day Six:** 20% old diet and 80% new food
- **Day Seven:** 100% new food

If you want to take a little longer, repeat each day's percentages twice, taking two weeks to transition your dog.

Monitor your dog carefully. If he suddenly refuses to eat or he has diarrhea or vomiting, slow down the transition even more. It doesn't matter how long it takes, so long as you do it safely. You should also contact your vet for advice if your dog's symptoms don't change.

Make sure you are not feeding your dog more than you normally would. Too much or too little food will affect your dog. Monitor your dog carefully for changes in weight. After a time, you will learn to adjust their food, based on weight changes, reactions, and nutritional requirements.

8. How Should Homemade Dog Food Be Stored?

In pretty much the same way as you would store your own food. Most homemade dog foods can be refrigerated for up to three days with no problem, although some treats can last longer, depending on what they are made of. You can also freeze the food in portions for up to three months. If you refrigerate food, store it in airtight containers, while freezer-safe containers or Ziploc bags can be used for frozen food.

BONUS: Should You Feed a BARF Diet?

Until now, most of the recipes you have been introduced to are cooked but what if you want to feed your dog a raw diet? You have undoubtedly heard of raw diets for dogs, specifically BARF.

BARF is a well-known acronym for Bones and Raw Food, although it is sometimes used for Biologically Appropriate Raw Food Diet. BARF is a way of feeding your dog a diet of raw muscle meats, meaty bones, organ meats, veggies, and fruits. It is a completely natural diet with no preservatives and nothing artificial.

A raw food diet can help improve your dog's health because they are high in protein and nutrients, at least much higher than any commercial feed. It is firmly based on the idea that our domesticated dog's ancestors were scavengers, living on a low-carb, high-protein diet with some plant-based ingredients. In short, BARF is a natural, wild-dog diet.

What Is in a BARF Diet?

A typical BARF diet is made up of the following raw ingredients:

- 70% muscle meat

- 10% meaty, edible bones

- 10% veggies and fruits

- 5% liver

- 5% other secreting organs, including brain, testicles, kidney, and spleen

Muscle meat is the best source of protein for a raw diet, as it contains the building blocks a dog needs – essential amino acids.

- **Proteins:** This includes lean beef, pork, or turkey, along with kidney, liver, and other organ meats. You can also provide raw meaty bones once per week, and raw whole eggs, including the shells.

- **Vegetables:** This includes raw cabbage, broccoli, pumpkin, squash, carrots, spinach, and other dark leafy greens. Do NOT feed onions, garlic, or avocado, as these are harmful.

- **Fruits:** This includes blueberries, cranberries, bananas, and apples, but avoid grapes and raisins as they are toxic to a dog's system.

- **Fresh Herbs:** You can also add fresh parsley, oregano, and basil to your dog's diet.

Like a cooked homemade diet, you must get everything right with a raw diet to ensure your dog has a nutritionally balanced diet.

Pros and Cons:

Feeding a raw diet provides plenty of health benefits:

- Better digestion
- Easier nutrient absorption
- Better energy levels
- More stamina
- Cleaner teeth
- Stronger bones
- Fresher breath
- Healthy coat and skin
- Less risk of allergies
- Better, healthier joints
- Weight management
- Less risk of cancer
- Smaller, less smelly stools

Most of these benefits are due to a BARF diet being high in natural calcium, omega fatty acids, glucosamine, and chondroitin sulfate. It is also free of preservatives, processed foods, and coloring agents and is naturally low-calorie.

The Risks

Like any diet, especially raw food, the BARF diet has potential risks. Before you opt for a raw diet, you must do your research, and you must talk to your vet. There are plenty of myths doing the rounds about BARF diets, not to mention a few misconceptions, too.

For example, some people think that raw diets are unhealthy and can cause food-borne illnesses in their dogs. Others think it's dangerous for a dog to eat a whole bone, believing it can lead to choking or harm their health in other ways. This may be true, so you should always give your dog a size-appropriate bone and supervise them when they eat them. Lastly, some people don't believe it is a properly balanced diet.

Regarding food-borne illness, all raw meat has bacteria, such as salmonella and E. coli, but these don't affect dogs as badly as humans. Food doesn't stay in a dog's system as long as it does in a human's either, so the bacteria aren't given the chance to grow, which means there's no time for them to cause disease. Done properly, a BARF diet is perfectly safe and healthy for your dog.

BARF diets are also well-balanced, provided they are prepared properly and include the nutrients your dog needs in the right amounts.

How to Prepare a BARF Diet

If you decide to try your dog on a BARF diet, you need to research and ensure you understand your dog's nutritional needs. The following tips will help you:

1. **Gradually Move Your Dog onto a Raw Diet:** Switching your dog from a commercial to a raw diet in one go can lead to discomfort for your dog. Like any diet, change it slowly, gradually replacing his normal diet with raw until he is fully transitioned.

2. **Don't Change Their Feeding Schedule:** If you normally feed your dog twice a day, stick to that. It's a routine they are used to, and changing it can affect your dog negatively. Work out how much raw food to feed them daily and divide between their normal number of meals.

3. **Always Weigh Food Portions:** A healthy adult dog should be fed 2 to 3% of their body weight per day. Watch your dog's weight – if they gain or lose weight, you will need to adjust portion sizes.

4. **Feed Your Dog Whole Meat Cuts:** You cut the meat into smaller pieces when you feed a cooked, homemade diet. It's best to leave the cuts as whole as possible with a raw diet. That way, your dog can digest the food better, and it helps their teeth stay clean.

5. **Variety Is Key:** Never feed your dog the same food every day for two reasons. First, they'll get bored, and second, they won't get a good enough range of nutrients. Rotate goods regularly, especially protein sources, and alternate between red meat, poultry, and fish.

6. **Feed Raw Bones, Never Cooked:** Raw bones are packed with nutrients and help keep teeth clean. If your dog is a small or toy breed, stick to smaller bones like chicken wings or necks, as large ones can create problems with the digestive system or cause choking. Cooked bones are a no-no, as they can splinter and cause internal damage. When you feed your dog bones, supervise them until they are finished eating.

7. **Include Veggies and Fruits:** Vegetables and fruits are a small but critical part of a raw diet, as they provide the minerals, vitamins, and antioxidants your

dog needs. Make them easier on your dog's digestive system by serving them pureed, grated, or chopped.

8. **Give Your Dog Some Dairy:** Include dog-safe cheese and yogurt to provide additional healthy nutrients.

9. **You May Need to Add Vitamin and Mineral Supplements:** You'll need to talk to your vet, but what supplements you give will depend on your dog's diet. Often, for a vitamin deficiency, adding some extra pureed fruits and veggies will do the trick, but get proper advice first.

10. **Always Feed Fresh Food:** You can freeze your dog's meals, but they must be thoroughly thawed before serving them. When you portion the food for freezing, always mark the container with the date – it will stay fresh for up to six months.

11. **Raw Food Must Be Stored Safely:** Never store it with other foods, as it can cause cross-contamination. Keep it on its own shelf at the bottom of the refrigerator, or freeze it. Wash your hands and every surface before and after handling and prepping raw meat.

12. **Keep an Eye on Your Dog's Stool:** This is often the first indication that the new diet isn't agreeable. When the stool is too soft, you need to consider changes to the ingredients. If your dog gets prolonged diarrhea, even after switching them back to their original diet, speak to a vet.

How to Transition Your Dog to a Raw Food Diet

Switching your dog to a new diet is not always easy, especially when you change from a commercial to a raw food diet. It can be done, though, provided you follow these tips:

1. **Start Small:** Substitute a small amount of their normal diet with raw and increase it gradually, over a week or so, to give your dog time to get used to it. This will also help your dog's digestive and gastrointestinal system to adjust.

2. **Ensure it is Nutritionally Balanced:** It must include the right variety of animal and plant ingredients to ensure a nutritional balance.

3. **Speak to Your Vet:** They can tell you exactly your dog's nutritional needs and how to feed a balanced diet.

4. **Add Lean Meats**: Too much fatty meat will lead to obesity and digestive issues, while lean meat is an essential protein source.

5. **Only Feed Raw Bones**: And ensure they have plenty of joints. Good choices include feet, necks, and tails.

6. **Research Healthy Ingredients:** Include whole eggs, turmeric, coconut oil, kelp, and so on, as these all benefit your dog's health.

If you are at all unsure, speak to an expert to find out what you should and shouldn't include.

Nutritional Raw Food Recipes

The following recipes will help you prepare a nutritionally balanced diet for your dog and give you a good starting point.

All of the recipes have the following timings:

- **Prep Time:** 25 minutes
- **Mixing Time:** 5 minutes

These times include preparing fruits and veggies and removing fat and ones from fish and meat.

Always serve these meals at room temperature, so if they have been refrigerated, make sure you take them out a few hours before you need them. You can also stir in a little warm water or salt-free broth to make the meal a little more appealing to your dog.

These meals should be stored in the fridge in airtight containers and will last for three days, while you can freeze them for up to three months. Always thaw frozen dog meals in the fridge overnight.

Raw Beef and Chicken Neck

Makes: 11.1 lb.

Ingredients:

- 2 lb. of 90% lean ground beef
- 3 lb. skinless chicken necks
- 1 lb. of beef liver
- 1 lb. of chicken hearts
- 1 lb. of beef hearts

- 10 eggs

- 8 ounces of broccoli

- 8 ounces of kale

- 8 ounces of dandelion greens

- 12 ounces of berries – blueberries, cranberries, raspberries, or blackberries (or a mixture)

- 3 tbsp of hemp hearts or hulled hemp seeds

- 1 tbsp of green-lipped mussel powder

- ½ tsp of Himalayan salt

Instructions:

1. Put the liver, heart, and neck through a meat grinder or chop it into very small pieces. Put it all in a bowl with the ground beef.

2. Crack the eggs into a blender and add the kale, greens, broccoli, seeds, berries, mussel powder and salt and puree to a smooth consistency.

3. Pour it into the bowl with meat and use clean hands or a wooden spoon to combine the mixture thoroughly.

4. Divide it into the right size portions for your dog and freeze it in Ziploc bags or freezer-safe containers.

Feeding Guidelines

As a rough guide, this recipe feeds the following:

- **10 lb. dog:** 21 days

- **25 lb. dog:** 10 to 11 days

- **50 lb. dog:** 6 days

- **75 lb. dog:** 4 to 5 days

- **100 lb. dog:** 4 days

Nutritional Information

- **Calories:** 491.1 per pound
- **Fat:** 54.67 g per kilogram
- **Calcium:** 3.89 g per kilogram
- **Phosphorus:** 3.31 g per kilogram
- **Potassium**: 2.30 g per kilogram
- **Sodium:** 0.86 g per kilogram
- **Magnesium:** 0.33 g per kilogram
- **Iron:** 25.55 mg per kilogram
- **Copper:** 9.20 mg per kilogram
- **Manganese**: 3.13 mg per kilogram
- **Zinc:** 26.75 mg per kilogram
- **Selenium:** 0.15 mg per kilogram

Raw Rabbit, Chicken and Beef

Makes: 5.1 pounds

Ingredients:

- 2 ½ lb. of rabbit (whole carcass)
- 1 lb. of chicken heart
- ¼ lb. of beef liver
- 4 eggs
- 8 ounces of broccoli

- ½ ounce of chopped spinach
- 6 ounces of berries – choose one or a mix of raspberries, blueberries, cranberries and blackberries
- ½ tsp of green-lipped mussel powder

Instructions:

1. Chop the rabbit into small chunks or put it through a meat grinder with the heart and liver. Put it in a large bowl.

2. Crack the eggs into a blender, add the berries, spinach, broccoli, and mussel powder, and blend to a puree.

3. Add it to the meat and combine until thoroughly mixed.

4. Portion it out and freeze it until needed.

Feeding Guidelines

As a rough guide, this recipe feeds the following:

- **10 lb. dog:** 8 days
- **25 lb. dog:** 4 days
- **50 lb. dog:** 2 to 3 days
- **75 lb. dog:** 2 days
- **100 lb. dog:** 1 ½ days

Nutritional Information

- **Calories:** 461.5 per pound
- **Fat:** 52.73 g per kilogram
- **Calcium:** 5.76 g per kilogram
- **Phosphorus:** 3.74 g per kilogram

- **Potassium**: 2.34 g per kilogram

- **Sodium:** 0.66 g per kilogram

- **Magnesium:** 0.30 g per kilogram

- **Iron:** 24.62 mg per kilogram

- **Copper:** 5.71 mg per kilogram

- **Manganese**: 2.83 mg per kilogram

- **Zinc:** 27.14 mg per kilogram

- **Selenium:** 0.28 mg per kilogram

Raw Pork and Fish

Makes: 11.3 lb.

Ingredients:

- 5 lb. of 96% lean ground pork

- 3 lb. of pork heart

- 1 lb. of pork liver

- 1 lb. of oily fish, i.e., mackerel, sardines, etc.

- 8 ounces of kale

- 5 ounces of broccoli

- 4 ounces of dandelion greens

- 12 ounces of berries – blueberries, cranberries, blackberries, cranberries

- 6 tbsp of seaweed calcium

- 3 tsp of wheat germ oil

- 1 tbsp of hemp hearts or hulled hemp seeds

- ½ tsp of Himalayan salt
- 1.37 g of kelp powder

Instructions:

1. Put the liver and heart through a grinder or chop them into very small pieces.
2. Put the broccoli, kale, dandelion greens, seaweed calcium, seeds, kelp, berries, wheat germ oil, and salt in a blender or food processor and puree.
3. Combine the puree with the ground pork and heart/liver mix until well mixed.
4. Divide into portions and freeze.

Feeding Guidelines

As a rough guide, this recipe feeds the following:

- **10 lb. dog:** 18 days
- **25 lb. dog:** 9 days
- **50 lb. dog:** 5 to 6 days
- **75 lb. dog:** 4 days
- **100 lb. dog:** 3 days

Nutritional Information

- **Calories:** 477.1 per pound
- **Fat:** 40.87 g per kilogram
- **Calcium:** 3.89 g per kilogram
- **Phosphorus:** 3.41 g per kilogram
- **Potassium**: 19.61 g per kilogram
- **Sodium:** 0.74 g per kilogram

- **Magnesium:** 50.13 g per kilogram

- **Iron:** 37.35 mg per kilogram

- **Copper:** 2.03 mg per kilogram

- **Manganese**: 1.39 mg per kilogram

- **Zinc:** 21.18 mg per kilogram

- **Selenium:** 0.25 mg per kilogram

Raw Boneless Turkey and Egg

Makes: 11 pounds

Ingredients:

- 5 lb. of 93% lean ground turkey

- 2 lb. of chicken hearts

- 1 lb. of beef liver

- 6 eggs

- 8 ounces of dandelion greens

- 8 ounces of broccoli

- 8 ounces of kale

- 12 ounces of berries – mixed or use blueberries

- 6 tbsp of bone meal or seaweed calcium

- 3 tbsp of ground pumpkin seeds

- 2 tsp of Himalayan salt

- ¼ tsp of kelp

Instructions:

1. Put the heart and liver through a grinder or chop them very small.

2. Crack the eggs into a blender and add the greens, broccoli, kale, berries, pumpkin seed, salt, bone meal, and kelp and puree.

3. Mix the puree with the chopped offal and the ground meat.

4. Divide into portions and freeze.

Feeding Guidelines

As a rough guide, this recipe feeds the following:

- **10 lb. dog:** 22 days
- **25 lb. dog:** 11 days
- **50 lb. dog:** 6 to 7 days
- **75 lb. dog:** 5 days
- **100 lb. dog:** 4 days

Nutritional Information

- **Calories:** 520 per pound
- **Fat:** 59.37 g per kilogram
- **Calcium:** 3.77 g per kilogram
- **Phosphorus:** 3.22 g per kilogram
- **Potassium**: 17.88 g per kilogram
- **Sodium:** 1.10 g per kilogram
- **Magnesium:** 47.22 g per kilogram
- **Iron:** 22.65 mg per kilogram

- **Copper:** 9.08 mg per kilogram

- **Manganese**: 3.06 mg per kilogram

- **Zinc:** 25.72 mg per kilogram

- **Selenium:** 0.13 mg per kilogram

Raw Boneless Beef and Egg

Makes: 11 pounds

Ingredients:

- 5 lb. of 90% lean ground beef

- 2 lb. of beef heart

- 1 lb. of beef liver

- 8 ounces of dandelion greens

- 8 ounces of broccoli

- 8 ounces of kale

- 12 ounces of blueberries or use a mix

- 5 tbsp of bone meal or seaweed calcium

- 2 tsp of wheat germ

- 2 tsp of Himalayan salt

- ¼ tsp of kelp

Instructions:

1. Grind or chop the liver and heart and add it to a bowl with the ground turkey.

2. Puree the rest of the ingredients and combine them with the meat.

---

3. Freeze in portions.

Feeding Guidelines

As a rough guide, this recipe feeds the following:

- **10 lb. dog:** 22 days
- **25 lb. dog:** 11 days
- **50 lb. dog:** 6 to 7 days
- **75 lb. dog:** 5 days
- **100 lb. dog:** 4 days

Nutritional Information

- **Calories:** 534.1 per pound
- **Fat:** 56.56 g per kilogram
- **Calcium:** 3.07 g per kilogram
- **Phosphorus:** 2.84 g per kilogram
- **Potassium**: 15.33 g per kilogram
- **Sodium:** 1.13 g per kilogram
- **Magnesium:** 38.61 g per kilogram
- **Iron:** 22.65 mg per kilogram
- **Copper:** 8.69 mg per kilogram
- **Manganese**: 1.92 mg per kilogram
- **Zinc:** 25.84 mg per kilogram
- **Selenium:** 0.15 mg per kilogram

How to Choose the Best Ingredients

Now that you have an idea of how to make great raw meals for your dog, you'll want to know how to choose the right ingredients. The first thing to remember is that the biggest ingredient is meat, so check your local area for an abattoir, meat processor, or farmer. Grocery store meat is fine but if you have a local farmer or butcher, you'll find it easier to get a wider choice of organ meats and more choice of other meats, too.

Make sure your meat content is no more than 20% fat. Prepackaged meats are usually labeled as a certain percentage lean, i.e., 90% lean. The remainder is fat content, so a 90% lean ground meat has 10% fat.

You also need to look at organ meats. Again, this is where having a good relationship with a local butcher comes in handy, as they can put aside what you need each week.

Always purchase the highest quality you can, not just in meat but in eggs, poultry, and other ingredients. If you feed your dog poor-quality food, you won't get any health benefits and can end up harming him instead. Where possible, buy organic or grass-fed meats, which are guaranteed to be free of growth hormones and antibiotics, have been raised on pastures, and have plenty of healthy fresh air.

Do not buy genetically modified foods – the same goes for your diet – as these are unhealthy. Organic foods are grown without the use of chemical pesticides and fertilizers and are not grown using GMO seeds. Clean food equals a healthy dog.

Conclusion

Thank you for reading *"Homemade Healthy Dog Food Cookbook: An Easy-to-Follow Guide and Collection of the Best Recipes to Make Your Dog Happy and Healthy."*

Homemade dog food isn't just another fad. Done right, it is the best way to feed your dog, ensuring your pal gets the right mix of nutrients to keep him healthy and free of disease. However, as you have learned, it is critical to ensure your dog is getting the right nutritional balance in his meals, or you can end up doing him more harm. Luckily, this is not difficult to work out and you'll soon be prepping meals without having to think about it. You do need to consider several factors: age, condition, health, etc., but virtually every dog will benefit from a homemade diet.

Chapter 1 discussed everything you need to know to get started. You learned why you should do it, the immense benefits to your dog, and what you should and shouldn't include in their meals. You got a handy set of conversion charts to work out what measurements to use, and you learned how to ensure you get the right ingredients.

Chapter 2 taught you how your dog's meals should be structured and how to get the nutritional balance right. You learned the common beginner mistakes you need to avoid, how to adjust meal sizes for different sizes and breeds of dog, and how to keep your dog at a healthy weight with some protein-packed, healthy recipes to give you a head start.

Chapter 3 provided you with plenty of quick recipes packed with nutrients, while Chapter 4 gavc you some delightful snacks and mcals for your young pup. Chapter 5 helped you decide what to feed your senior dog, while Chapter 6 was all about grain-free meals for dogs with allergies.

In Chapter 7, you got some cool recipes for holiday and celebration treats for your pup – why should they be left out while you are tucking into your Thanksgiving or Christmas meal? Chapter 8 discussed homemade healthy supplements you can add to your dog's meals and Chapter 9 is all about tasty recipes to stuff a Kong toy with to keep your dog occupied.

Chapter 10 answered some of the more common questions people ask about making food for their dogs, while the final bonus chapter introduced you to the BARF diet and offered a few recipes to help you decide if a raw diet would suit your dog better.

Feeding your dog homemade food will provide benefits above anything you ever imagined, but you should consult your vet or a veterinary nutritionist first, just so they can talk you through what to do and make sure your dog is getting the right nutrition to ensure they grow up happy and healthy.

Thank you once again for reading this book, and if you enjoyed it, please can you leave a review – it doesn't just help authors, it helps other people decide if this is the book for them.

References

3 Reasons to Cook Your Own Dog Food. (n.d.). Www.thewildest.com. https://www.thewildest.com/dog-nutrition/reasons-make-your-own-dog-food

20 Essential Tools and Equipment. (2021, November 3). Dailydogfoodrecipes.com. https://dailydogfoodrecipes.com/tools-and-equipment/

Allrecipes. (2019). *Allrecipes | Food, friends, and recipe inspiration.* Allrecipes. https://www.allrecipes.com/

Basic Cooking Measurements & Handy Kitchen Conversion Chart (FREE!). (2017, July 6). The Cookie Rookie®. https://www.thecookierookie.com/cooking-measurements-kitchen-conversion-chart/

Benefits Of Fresh Dog Food: 10 Research-Backed Reasons To Switch. (2021, July 6). Tips, Advice & Stories for Dog Owners - Dog Eared. https://blog.myollie.com/health-benefits-of-fresh-natural-diet-for-dogs/

Dog Meals and Breeds: How Often Should Dogs Eat? (2023, June 19). Https://Gullyroad.com.au/. https://gullyroad.com.au/meal-sizes-and-times-for-your-dog-breed/

FAQ on Homemade Diets. (2010, July 28). Havanese Forum. https://www.havaneseforum.com/threads/faq-on-homemade-diets.1977/

Feeding and Treating Tips. (n.d.). Pet Food Institute. https://www.petfoodinstitute.org/pet-well-being/health-well-being/feeding-and-treating-tips/

Feedy, S. (n.d.). *BARF Diet for Dogs: A Complete Guide.* Super Feedy. https://superfeedy.com/blogs/news/barf-diet-for-dogs-a-complete-guide

Food, K. B. P. (n.d.). *How to Make Homemade Dog Food.* Know Better Pet Food. https://www.knowbetterpetfood.com/blogs/blog/how-to-make-homemade-dog-food

Healing Golden Turmeric Paste Recipe For Your Dog. (2015, April 28). Www.dogsnaturallymagazine.com. https://www.dogsnaturallymagazine.com/healing-with-turmeric-golden-paste-for-dogs/

Homemade Dog & Cat Food Recipes. (2021, July 17). Pawsome Recipes. https://pawsomerecipes.com/

Homemade Dog Food: Is It Healthy to Cook for Your Dog? (n.d.). Www.petmd.com. https://www.petmd.com/dog/nutrition/how-make-sure-your-homemade-dog-food-delivers-right-nutrients

Live Eat Learn - Easy vegetarian recipes, one ingredient at a time. (2017, March 25). Live Eat Learn. https://www.liveeatlearn.com/

nagi. (2018, December 13). *RecipeTin Eats - A Food Blog Serving Up Quick & Easy Dinner Recipes.* RecipeTin Eats. https://www.recipetineats.com/

Nov 22, I. P. P. P., Sep 27, 2021 | 4 M. U., & 2023. (n.d.). *Homemade Dog Food Recipes: Choosing Balanced Ingredients.* American Kennel Club. https://www.akc.org/expert-advice/nutrition/choosing-ingredients-homemade-dog-food/

Randall, S. (2022, April 21). *FAQ: 12 Most Common Questions I'm Asked About Homemade Dog Food.* https://topdogtips.com/common-homemade-dog-food-questions/

Spies, D. (2021, July 23). *30-Minute Stovetop Homemade Dog Food «Healthy DIY Recipe.* Clean & Delicious. https://cleananddelicious.com/homemade-dog-food/

What Are the Best Ingredients For Homemade Dog Food? | Petfinder. (n.d.). Www.petfinder.com. https://www.petfinder.com/dogs-and-puppies/feeding/food-and-treats/best-ingredients-homemade-dog-food/

Printed in Great Britain
by Amazon

58003485R00119